FROM VALOR TO VIRTUE

The Moral Development
of the Brave

Father Michael Pacella III

urbanpress

WHAT OTHERS ARE SAYING ABOUT FATHER MICHAEL PACELLA AND HIS WORK AMONG LAW ENFORCEMENT AND MILITARY OFFICIALS.

**From Bishop Michael Davidson,
pastor of The Cathedral Church of the King in Olathe, Kansas,
and Father Pacella's presiding bishop:**

It is a great honor to have the opportunity to write a character reference for Father Michael Pacella.

As his Bishop, I have had the privilege to work with Father Michael for some nine years. I have seen him persevere through many challenges in pursuing his doctorate and in church planting. He and his wife Doreen have endured many setbacks, but they keep on keeping on! He never quits, no matter what.

They have adopted children and experienced the loss of one of their daughters. Yet they continue to minister to others. Father Michael is deeply involved as a chaplain at William and Mary College in Williamsburg, VA, and in working with the police department on campus. In this role he has again experienced many sorrowful encounters. In spite of his personal losses, he stands his post and serves others.

Father Michael lives what he writes! Someone has said that sorrow is life's greatest teacher. You can see this coming true in his life. Out of many sorrows, Father Michael has been able to tap into the mystery of suffering and show how this forms the heart of the brave. He is a true hero, since he responds in a moment of time to needs greater than his own!

I highly recommend everyone to read everything Father Michael writes. You will find strength for your soul in the midst of a troubled world. Your heart will expand, be enlarged, and you will run in the path of the Lord's command because He has set your heart free (see Psalm 119:32).

From Joseph B. St. John, retired law enforcement officer and administrator for 30 years:

Over the years, I have had the opportunity to watch Father Mike's presentations to law enforcement officers and college students regarding ethics. On the surface, ethics seems like such an easy topic. It is just a straightforward subject on what is right and what is wrong. However, nothing could be further from the truth.

Father Mike can peel the topic back and expose the real meaning of ethics in all its complexity and he forces the listener to confront the true meaning of ethics. With a quick wit and attention to details, Father Mike has the ability to draw the student in and help them rethink their own positions on this important topic.

I also had the opportunity to be Father Mike's student. Each class was a fascinating journey into the importance of questioning everything that you think about and accept as truth. He held each student's attention for weeks, as we discussed the importance of man, God, and ultimately morality, especially in regard to law enforcement ethics.

Father Mike's class taught me a lot about life and about living. He has grown from being a teacher to me, to be a mentor, and finally, a friend. He truly is a man for our current season, a man who understands ethics but more importantly understands *why* ethics matter.

From Hank Smith, Mindfaith Ministries board member, longtime friend, and businessman:

Having known Father Michael for the past 16 years, originating with our service together in a helicopter aviation battalion in the U.S. Army in South Korea, I have seen and experienced firsthand both his example and passion for those who choose to serve in uniform in any capacity. Like others, I understand some of the unique scenarios that create dilemmas that have challenged me to the core of my being, as I have strived to serve the public good and my teams with integrity. Father Michael has been a most excellent in-the-moment resource for me, whether it be in observation of his excellent character in action with others or in intimate conversations addressing challenging questions needed to deliver the most morally responsible leadership to my teams.

ISBN 978-1-63360-059-1
For Worldwide Distribution
Printed in the U.S.A.

Urban Press
P.O. Box 8881
Pittsburgh, PA 15221-0881
412.646.2780
www.urbanpress.us

CONTENTS

PREFACE

I have had the privilege of knowing Father Michael Pacella III for more than 18 years, starting with his days as an Army chaplain. During that time, I have followed the development of his ideas about morality and ethics for those entrusted with the use of force. The role of Christians in the military serving in war has always created controversy because they carry weapons for the purpose of killing their enemies, while the commandment from God states that "Thou shalt not kill." The actual Hebrew word translates both into kill or murder, English words that differentiate between justified and unjustified homicide. Still, it creates a dilemma for those who bear arms, and many who kill in war still suffer from guilt. Having served as a chaplain with the airborne and special operations community at Fort Bragg, North Carolina, Father Pacella encountered the elite of the military. While the vast majority of men and women serve out of a sense of patriotism or fulfilling a family tradition of military service, the elite seek out the challenge of combat. They strive to perfect themselves in the use of weapons of war.

From this elite environment, he then became an instructor and chaplain in the Army Transportation School, where he taught ethics to and nurtured the spirit of those soldiers who served to serve others. While there, our nation began its Global War on Terror and he came in contact with a new generation of warriors. The experience of war changes people, some for the good and others struggle with the horror of it. It was at the Transportation School that I coincidently was conducting research into the experience of truck drivers defending their convoys against enemy attacks in Vietnam, Iraq, and Afghanistan. Our parallel research led to enlightening discussions. This assignment also gave him time to articulate his ideas on morality and ethics in the military, which led to a calling to pursue his PhD and teach theology. After leaving the Army, he has worked with police officers and found many similarities in the moral and ethical challenges faced by them and the military in combat. During this time, we have remained friends and our conversations on the subject of morality and ethics in war and peace have continued.

Father Pacella has developed an incredible insight into the world of those who bear arms with the responsibility to keep our nation's enemies at bay and keeping our citizens safe on the streets at home. Understanding the great moral and ethical challenges they face, he realizes that the solution is internal, not just external. Rules do not always provide the right solution for every situation. An answer must be found from within, based upon a good moral foundation and respect for human dignity. In a life where people are divided into sheep, wolves, and sheep dogs, Father Pacella has articulated a path for those empowered with the responsibility of wielding force.

Now, more than ever, there is a need for a study on the ethical use of power and authority. Law enforcement has recently come under greater scrutiny for the killings in the line of duty, leaving many to question whether shooting to kill was the appropriate resort and for soldiers, the proper escalation of force. Those empowered with authority and the power to take life need a training program for their moral conscience that will provide them the right answers when needed. This book, and the instruction that Father Pacella provides in his seminars and workshops, should be a part of the training for all those who bear arms in the area of ethics and moral development.

Richard Killblane
US Army Transportation Corps Historian and Author
Williamsburg, VA

INTRODUCTION

I started the book you hold in your hand in 2007 and finalized it in 2013. I began by using the material I will present in many university lectures as well as in seminars and workshops at police academies and for police advanced training. It was there that I saw how relevant the material was, as I received feedback from those who heard my lectures and began to put what they heard into practice. It is obvious from recent headlines that the need for this material is greater now more than ever. The issue is that we, as a society, and specifically in our military and law enforcement work, must grow in moral excellence. What's more, the premise of this book is that this growth *can* take place once we believe it is possible and begin to pursue it proactively.

Before I go on, I want to acknowledge several people who have encouraged me along the way. I thank Professor John Delos for his patient reading and re-reading of my material. His friendship has been an invaluable asset in my life, and I was grateful that he included me as a guest lecturer in one of his courses. I have learned so much from him. Thank you, Paisano! My thanks also go out to Richard K. Killblane for his tireless encouragement and help (he is an excellent writer and teacher) and to Hank Smith, a dear friend who is always available to talk. Hank, your wisdom and insight are treasured more than you know.

Most of all, I want to acknowledge my wife of 43 years— Doreen Ann. I married well, and Doreen has constantly challenged me during our entire journey together, while supporting me as I have lived out my dreams. Thank you, Doreen, for your many sacrifices and unwavering love. You are truly a heavenly treasure and the love of my life!

A project of this magnitude, especially in the face of hostile and conflicting cultural values, is not an easy task. What makes it even more difficult is the ubiquitous social media and other media outlets that have made the recent moral failures of those in law enforcement available to the public in real time. As you read, please keep in mind that I do not pretend to have arrived and now all the reader has to do is catch up with me. I, too, am in the development process and the governing principles I will outline in this book are challenging me, since I fall short of living them out on a day-to-day basis. The process of drudgery—discipline—delight (also called the 3D process) is always at work in my life.

This 3D process can be compared to what a long-distance runner goes through. If you begin to develop the habit of running (it will take about twenty-one days if you are consistent), it will at first be drudgery, no matter what the running magazines try to tell you or how great the equipment is that you buy. Second, it will become a discipline—a conditioning that goes beyond drudgery and becomes second nature, as you embrace training that is consistently done and not just talked about. Finally, the drudgery and the discipline transform into a delight when the habit has been acquired. The same is true for those who desire to grow in virtue. It requires work that eventually transitions into discipline but ends with a sense of delight. In a way, we are talking about moral transformation, as the 3D process is engaged and allowed to take its course.

There will be examples throughout the book but, for now, let's consider the concept of lying. If we are talking about moral transformation, it is not enough that a liar stop lying. That liar must form a new habit to replace the old one. Speaking the truth must become the new, improved habit, and anything less would be considered a failure. The objective can be nothing short of transformation of the liar, if we are talking about moral development.

I would like to express my highest esteem for the soldiers

of our country, of whom my son Michael IV was one, and to all the police personnel with whom I have had the privilege to work with over the last ten years. I feel a great burden and have a heavy heart, in light of the current events in our country, as they pertain to "police brutality" and civic unrest. I offer this manual that focuses on the moral development of individuals who are placed in positions of authority and great responsibility as my contribution to the worthy work that is already being done, day in and day out, in this country and beyond. To my fellow soldiers and law enforcement personnel, I would say without any hesitation that you have the valor. My goal is to equip you with the means to obtain the virtue, so that you are not incomplete heroes.

The research on this work has been going on for at least two decades, and was acquired when I was a U.S. Army chaplain (1995-2005) and a police chaplain (2004 to the present). There was a slight overlap in my service between the two, but it was a smooth transition due to the similar cultures in the two areas of work. I also have a post-graduate research degree from Harvard University in Ethics, which uniquely equipped me to examine the scenarios presented in this book with some measure of proficiency.

I have had top-rated, high-ranking professionals in the field, both in the military as well as in the police community here in the United States and in the United Kingdom, review this material and offer helpful suggestions. I have tested the research in police academy venues and in advanced training for police supervisors, and have received positive feedback. Most of the seminars (and I have conducted five to date) were eight-hour blocks of instruction with many practical exercises included.

There are many suggestions about what it will take for a more civil exchange to occur between those in power who are protecting us and those who are recipients of the protection being provided. The easy way is to change policy and not deal with the necessity of virtue being present in those who wield so much power. I offer a lasting solution that will take a great deal more effort than just attending a few classes. What's more, the declining moral nature of our Western societies in general will make the goal of moral transformation in law and military personnel that much more challenging, but it can and must be achieved. Aristotle taught the concepts of habit and internalization. That is what will be required for us to see lasting change in our cultural ethics in any field of endeavor.

As I write, I will often use the pronoun "we" when presenting examples to help understand and apply the material. I do that because I consider myself a part of law enforcement. I am a police chaplain for the William and Mary College Police Department, and ride with the officers on their rounds. I have gone to crime scenes with them and have often counseled them on the spot and after the fact, due to the gruesome or redundant nature of the work. The police officers are my colleagues and a few are friends, and I consider it an honor to work alongside them.

At the same time, I do not face what these men and women face every day. I stand with and help them where I can, but they are in the field every day. The same was true when I was a military chaplain. I was there, but I was not carrying a weapon. There are things I can relate to in both worlds (police and military), but I am not an expert. I am there to serve, and my service is limited to my role as a chaplain.

I have added some questions at the end of each chapter for several reasons. I can picture some police personnel reading this book in their vehicles (while parked, of course), and the questions can help them summarize what they have read, think about it, and perhaps even talk it over with their partner. The questions can also help with small group discussions that may emerge formally or informally, as professionals gather to talk about their work and what they are learning from this book.

My hope is that you will be open to the possibilities of

what I present in this book—that professionals can morally develop and transform through knowledge, effort, and hard work. I know we will never be perfect, but that does not excuse us from pursuing perfection. I pray this presentation will help us develop the virtue that must go along with the valor.

Father Michael Pacella III
Williamsburg, VA
June 2019

CHAPTER 1

THE MYSTERY

OF VIRTUE

ISN'T SO MYSTERIOUS

The concepts of moral capacity and moral development are directly related to the belief that any person can improve in the practice of what has been historically known as virtue. Virtue is defined as "conformity to a standard of right or morality." My stated premise throughout this book is this: There is no limit to the moral development that can take place in a reasonable person, once that person is cognizant of his or her moral capacity. *Virtue ethics*, the category of ethics that addresses this phenomenon, starts with the notion of moral expectations and moral obligations, even in a non-religious setting, and asserts that this capacity and development are possible.

Of course, there are several components that must be present for this moral development to occur. First, there must be the desire for change, transformation, and growth. Second, there must an honest assessment of the current reality that exists in any person or group desiring this change. Third, there must be the visualization of the end result—the person or group pursuing the change must know what the change looks like.

Habit is something that is integral to our discussion of moral development. Interestingly, Aristotle emphasized habit as a means to moral development. Saint Thomas Aquinas also used this concept as the means for the possible development of virtue in any human being. The fact that "saints" have reached a level of maturity through the regimen or habits of holiness indicates that, if given the chance, moral development can take place in almost anyone who desires it. Although this statement may seem highly speculative to some, there is too much empirical evidence in the history of the Christian church to believe otherwise.

The physical capacity that ultra-marathon runners have exhibited, along with the mental capacity that scholars have acquired, has begged the question concerning the moral capacity of human beings: What is our moral capacity for good? An excuse system that explains away or excuses immoral behavior by saying, "I am only human," ignores or underestimates the moral capacity that humans possess. My work with soldiers and police personnel has strengthened my conviction that this moral capacity theory is achievable and demonstrable. People in law enforcement and the military have the capacity, if they have the desire, to achieve and exhibit a high level of moral development.

With the call for the re-training of police officers due to the recent high-profile of negative "over-reactions" to situations, perhaps this basic premise of moral development should be given more thought and attention. It is my hope this book will provide the necessary framework that will prove a higher moral development is possible and will give some suggestions for training possibilities.

From Valor to Virtue

The title of this book is *From Valor to Virtue*. The question we will examine is: Can those who are brave, who protect our freedoms and our way of life, also be paragons of virtue, honesty, and integrity? In Western culture, where development in every realm has flourished, I would like to propose another related question: Why has there not been a greater emphasis on moral development?

In the physical realm, men and women have accomplished great feats. Consider again, the example of the endurance of marathon runners. Men and women have run hundreds of miles over a period of days in grueling conditions and have gone far beyond what was thought "possible." In the intellectual realm, outstanding discoveries have been made that prove the exceptional mental capacity of humankind. In the U.S. Army, I was challenged "to be all I could be." The Army believed I possessed the potential to develop physically, professionally, and ethically/spiritually, a concept popularly known as "total fitness." Yet, there was limited emphasis and training to develop the moral side of the soldier who would be called upon to make life-altering decisions in an instant.

In the twentieth century, the moral development of the brave and in our society as a whole has seemed to have lost its underpinnings, with the exception of a few isolated cases, such as Mother Saint Teresa. Part of the problem of low moral results has to do with a lack of understanding the concept of *moral capacity*. The other part of the problem has to do with expectations, for if we do not expect that mankind *can* improve, then we will not even pursue or expect the possibility. These issues and many others must be addressed if the present-day culture is going to deal successfully with the ills of society. We are in desperate need of moral development, but we are stuck because we don't emphasize it or believe it to be possible. "Stuck" is probably not the right word, for our moral condition is not stable but digressing.

Many people equate moral development or virtue with organized religion, which is not the case. What I am presenting is not a religious proposal, for when we compare the higher rational animal (man) with lower level animals, we see that moral decisions are part of everyone's life. A dog does not have to decide whether or not to rob a bank, only a human has to grapple with that moral issue. A cat does not have to wrestle with the issue of divorce, but humans regularly and (unfortunately) increasingly face that issue.

Humans are not solely instinctual animals, but rational beings that can do good. A horse did not develop a procedure for a heart transplant. A goldfish does not send help to an area ravaged by floods. What's more, it is not only "church" people who do those "good" things for individuals or society. Humans have the capacity to do good, just like they do to run fast or think well. Both capacities must be developed if they are to become all that they can be. Unfortunately, we have chosen to develop the runners and honor the academics, while ignoring the moralists.

More than that, history is on the side of the existence and potential for moral development. It is only recently that we have seen a moral decline, for up until that point, there were startling examples of virtue in many cultures, with or without religion. Church involvement, along with moral philosophy and theology, enhance moral development, but even human anthropology un-aided by God's grace is capable of doing good things. We have the capacity to do good since we are made in the image of God, and that capacity is dormant until we choose to breathe life into it through proactive development.

Most of my experience associated with this project has been gained with soldiers and police personnel over more than a decade. In the process, I have established a program, which I will refer to as the Moral Vocabulary for Police Personnel. This program has provided police personnel with the vocabulary to help them understand the moral terrain they are called to uphold and sometimes define. The language used in this research, for the most part, is non-religious; the concepts, however, are rooted in moral philosophy and theology, time-tested governing principles that have proven effective in the realm of moral development.

The moral language starts with the basic concept of

blushing. It is an indicator of moral maturity. It ends with other various principles of virtue. Blushing is the first moral indicator, a physiological response to the recognition that we have done something wrong. Consider Hamlet's words, when considering the motives for his mother's hurried marriage to his father's murderer: "O shame! Where is thy blush?"

The process of moving toward virtue is grueling and, as a result, can be quite appealing to personnel who esteem discipline as a part of their profession, as indicated by a quote from Simonides (560-468 BC): "Virtue lives on a high rock painful to climb and guarded by a band of pure and evasive nymphs. No mortal may look upon her unless sweat pours from his body and he climbs the summit of manliness."

When I talk to police personnel, I emphasize that moral development is hard work. Without it, they will be morally challenged while valorous stalwarts. This resonates with them because they are accustomed to the hard work required to hone their skills in the areas of marksmanship, martial arts, and crisis intervention. I try to instill in them the need to put the same emphasis on their moral development, as I did for military personnel.

Before we proceed, a more complete definition of virtue is in order to further our understanding. "Virtue is a word formed from the Latin *virtus*, which means power or strength or valor or manliness." One reason that virtue continues to evade many people is that moral development programs have often deemphasized the fact that constant effort is required.

A pastor once presented the best metaphor I ever heard to describe the nature of effort involved in moral development. He referred to it as "swimming in peanut butter." His point was that moral development requires persistent effort with sometimes little progress. This concept of continual effort is not new and can be traced back to Aristotle. The plan I have developed gives a practical route for modern individuals to follow.

It is helpful to distinguish between *moral formation* and

moral information to avoid the production of moral-stunted people. Sometimes when people hear a truth, they believe they have assimilated that truth. Of course, that is not necessarily the case. To affirm the truth but not apply truth is where moral growth can be stunted or prevented altogether. How does anyone know when they are developing morally? Aristotle had the answer when he wrote in his work, *Ethics*, that "pleasure in doing virtuous acts is a sign that the virtuous disposition has been acquired." Knowledge alone cannot produce the pleasure of which Aristotle spoke.

The journey that leads from being valiant to being valiant and virtuous is long and hard, and few travel it. It may be that the maps are out of date or that those who have traveled it are not available any longer as guides. Whatever the obstacles there are to overcome, this journey must be explored and experienced, so that others can make the trip as well. That is what I propose to do in this book: Construct a map for intentional moral and ethical development aimed at law enforcement and military professionals, to prove that moral development is necessary and attainable by God's grace and design. With that goal in mind, let's get started. We'll start where I often begin, and that is with a definition of the terms often associated with the pursuit of moral awareness and development.

CHAPTER 2

LEARNING YOUR

MORAL VOCABULARY

Before we proceed, perhaps it would be beneficial to provide a glossary that includes what I refer to as a moral vocabulary. We will refer to these concepts throughout this book, so it will be good if you familiarize yourself with them now. You didn't even know there was a moral vocabulary, did you? That's good, because it shows you the need to study and learn more, so you can grow in your understanding. The following is a list comprised of 35 categories that must be present if a meaningful understanding of and dialogue in moral development are to be achieved. Let me go through the list and provide a brief description of each category.

Some of these words are perhaps familiar words outside of a moral context. Within the framework that I am writing, however, they must be understood in a broader sense. They make up the terrain of the moral order, an order with which most people are not familiar. I will try to handle each of them with simple clarity.

Blushing
Blushing is a moral barometer of sorts. If one cannot

blush, it is an indicator of a perceived moral lapse of which that person is aware. Blushing is common to most people, and is uncontrollable when it happens. It is interesting to note that animals do not blush. What's more, our faces blush, as opposed to our hands. Our moral lapse shows forth for all to see! When blushing is ignored and the behavior continues, it will cause a hardening of the heart that can lead to moral insensitivity, which leads to even more regular and egregious moral lapses.

Social Norms

Social norms are normal behavior accepted by a society at large. For example, urinating in public is not acceptable in the American culture, but it is more acceptable or at least tolerated in other cultures. Every culture has a general idea of what normal behavior is. For example, no culture honors murder, rape, lying, or theft. When people deny the basic reality of this awareness of normal, they begin to see agreement concerning what is acceptable behavior around social norms rather than morality. This is a mistake.

Normal behavior emanates from the concept of universals (to be discussed below). Remember, ethics is a branch of philosophy that seeks to understand the nature, purposes, justification for, and founding principles of moral rules. Morality is a class of rules held by society to govern the right conduct of its members, so that there can be such a thing as social norms.

Golden Mean

Golden mean is a term coined by Aristotle (or at least used by him) to express moderation. It is the balance between two extremes. Cowardice is the extreme on one side and recklessness is the other extreme on the other, so, therefore, courage would be considered the golden mean between those two. Another example would be the virtue of generosity. On the one hand, if people are miserly, they are considered stingy. If they give everything away, they are considered excessive, wasteful, and irresponsible. The golden mean in that scenario is generosity, for generous people are not holding on to what they have that others need and are not giving away what their families need.

Golden Rule

The Golden Rule is a concept attributed to Jesus, but the principle existed prior to his usage. The meaning is also referred to as the law of reciprocity in that you would do to others as you would have them do to you. It is referred to as the law of reaping and sowing. If you want to be treated well, treating others in that same fashion would be an expression of the Golden Rule.

Values

Values represent what is most important in our lives, such as family, freedom, and our faith. We invest time and money into these esteemed behaviors and principles, and are willing to defend and even go to war to defend our values. We often say we value certain things, and those are the priorities we follow in our behaviors and actions. When we do not devote ourselves to these things, however, we indicate that those things are not truly values, but rather preferences that are important, but not vital, to our existence. Values are an indication of what we truly cherish.

Universals

We alluded to universals under the concept of social norms. Universals are internationally-agreed-upon social norms. We use this concept as a basis for the Law of War or what is commonly known as International Law. The Hague and Geneva Conventions are based on the understanding that universals of right and wrong exist and are consistent in almost all cultures, and people can be held accountable by the rest of the world for behavior inconsistent with those universals. These universals govern the treatment of prisoners of war and the rules of combat. The very definition of war crimes has as its foundation a common sense of decency that would be drawn from universals.

Rule-Keeping

Rule-keeping is what is commonly known as "playing fair," according to a set of agreed-upon rules. This category is for the morally underdeveloped who must have a set of guidelines to follow in order to exhibit fair play and justice. Keeping rules, however, does not indicate that internalization of virtue has occurred. If the rules are withdrawn, the undesirable behavior may return or persist. Children keep rules but adults cultivate virtue. Following rules is a good place to begin, but moral development must progress beyond rules to be able to judge appropriate moral actions when there are only moral principles (and no rules) to govern and guide a situation at hand.

Conscience

Conscience is a word that describes the "inner voice" of one's moral formation. It is an indicator that tells individuals their actions are violating their core values and thus hindering their moral formation. When people say their conscience is bothering them, they mean that their actions and moral disposition are in conflict. The conscience must be informed and formed. It does not replace the "voice of God." It is not infallible, but most of the time should be obeyed, and when violated can often be the source of blushing or uneasy feelings.

It is quite possible for some to ignore their conscience, and it is possible for a "sensitive" conscience to alert a person to a problem or shortcoming that does not exist—but it does exist in the mind of the beholder, even if no one else can see the situation that caused the violation of conscience. For example, someone may "feel bad" when they do not speak to someone who was at a party with them. The reality could be that both people were so distracted or busy that it was physically impossible to greet. Yet the one person may have a twinge of conscience, where others would say, "There was no problem because there was no way to talk." The offender may still "feel badly," because he or she violated a personal value of verbally greeting all friends to acknowledge their friendship.

Natural Law

Natural law is a philosophical term that describes the transcendent law within each person that enables them to instinctively know right and wrong. A natural law is inherent in human nature. For example, the Founding Fathers appealed to natural law in their rejection of oppression by a monarch that included taxation without representation. Slavery is another good (or perhaps bad) example of this reality. Laws and even "apparent" biblical justification could not convince people that slavery was justified because of the existence of natural law.

Dr. King, in his *Letter from a Birmingham Jail*, referenced Augustine and Aquinas when he wrote, "an unjust law is no law at all." Dr. King was acknowledging that laws were made to legalize slavery and racial oppression, but those laws violated natural law that operated in all people. This is why so many caricatures of African-Americans portray them in hideous forms. That was done so the oppressors could justify their violation of natural law by attempting to show the oppressed as less than human. If they had not done that, natural law would have screamed out against their oppression of a fellow human being.

Moral Law

Moral law is the source of civil law, as expressed in many of the state laws of the Thirteen Colonies. It is never based on the whims or opinions of the populace. People do not vote in a democratic sense to agree on moral law. The prohibition of murder and rape are civil laws, which have been derived from the moral law taken from the Ten Commandments in the Old Testament. They are transcendent principles that come not from the state, but from God.

Not every law is based on morality, contrary to the arguments made by some who try to broaden the concept of morality. Just because something is legal does not automatically mean it is moral, and businesses must face this issue regularly. It may not be against civil law to pollute, but it actually may be a violation of moral law that God's creation is to be respected and cared for. It may be civil law, but it is never moral law to enslave other people, regardless of the economic value the enslavement provides to the social order. A highway speed limit is not a moral law, but is based on a number of reasons that achieve a prescribed end.

Physical Law(s)

Physical laws are clearly the laws of nature that will not or cannot be defied or denied. They are laws like gravity, the rising of the sun, and the changing of the seasons, and they operate regardless of the circumstances and apart from the will of man. I will show later in this book how moral laws work in the same way as physical laws. It doesn't matter if someone believes in the law of gravity or not. If they jump from the 20th story of a building, they will fall, and probably to their death. Moral laws operate in the same manner, for someone may not believe they exist, but when they are broken, there are consequences.

Civil Law

Civil laws are man-made laws rooted in the moral law. Civil law is not created by moral consensus—people agreeing on what is right and wrong. It provides the state with civility, and is where we obtain our word *civilization*. We base civil law on the natural and moral laws that exist in nature and in the hearts of people. Sometimes a law is a just law and at other times a law is unjust. The determining factor is how the law squares with God's law—if it does, then it can be considered just.

Professional Ethics

Professional ethics is a code of behavior that guides professionals in their behaviors and actions. It is exclusively external, and may not necessarily be a part of the moral fabric of the individual. For example, accountants have professional ethics that guide the way they report income, expenses, assets, and liabilities. The attorney-client privilege that guarantees confidentiality is a matter of professional ethics, as are the rules that govern the behavior of doctors and dentists.

Revealed Law

Revealed law is a theological term that describes the behavior required by God as revealed in His sacred Law. An example of this would be one of the Ten Commandments (also known as the Decalogue), "Thou shall not steal." Revealed law would and could not be known without some special acts of God to reveal that law, and those Ten Commandments were delivered to Moses on Mt. Sinai as a special revelation of God's will.

Unwritten Law

Unwritten laws are tacit codes that are understood, although seldom, if ever, verbalized. The unwritten laws can almost become sacred among families and people groups. These "laws" are clearly-understood expectations and are adhered to with a loyalty that is unmatched by people outside the immediate group. In my Italian family, the unwritten law was that we were to be engaged by the age of 21, married by 22, and the intended spouse was to be an Italian. Another example would be gang members who are expected to be loyal to one another, not betraying a fellow member to the law or any other agency.

When Americans stand and place their hand over their heart at the playing of the National Anthem, they are exhibiting an unwritten law in action. No one would be arrested or fined for not standing, but the cultural expectation is so powerful that few can oppose it, as evidenced by the current protests going on in the National Football League.

Virtue Ethics

Virtue ethics is a category of ethics that highlights virtue as the manifestation of the "good life." Aristotle expressed the need for virtue (sharing the same values) to be present for friendships to exist with any kind of longevity. Virtue ethics is a complex issue best described by the following series of statements:

1. Virtue is a habit—a firm inward determination to do good.
2. The human virtues are dispositions of the intellect and will that direct our acts, prioritize our passions, and persuade our conduct.
3. The moral virtues grow through instruction, intentional acts, and deliberate attention given to their exercise.
4. Virtue comes from the Latin word *virtus*, which can mean power or strength. It takes effort and strength to acquire and maintain virtue.
5. The unvirtuous do not esteem virtue since they do not value it, so therefore they do not pay attention to its cultivation.

These references are important to know if we are going to understand the nature of virtue. The discipline called *virtue ethics*, when compared to something like professional ethics, has more to do with internalization of values and development of moral fiber. It is not conformity to an external standard only, but instead it is a determination to work on one's interior life.

Moral Reasoning

Moral reasoning is the highest faculty of the soul, according to some ancient moral philosophers. Most people are capable of processing moral content in their intellect and then directing their wills with clarity to carry out moral actions. The moral parameters provided by philosophers and theologians enable this exercise to occur. Moral reasoning provides moral parameters that will establish moral guidelines for reasonable ethical deliberation.

Moral Capacity

Moral capacity is the capability that reasonable people have to be cognizant and measure their moral development and their need for moral growth. Consider marathon runners in training. They know how far they can run, and are aware of what they need yet to do to finish a 26-mile race. That is how a person would approach their moral capacity as well. What is your moral IQ? Have you ever even considered that component of your holistic development?

Moral Development

Moral development is the growth that takes place when one is trained in the arena of morality. This development must be intentional or it will not occur. It represents what people can do, once they are cognizant of their moral capacity. Moral development, like any other physical or skill development, is progressive. Any development requires measurement and that is a challenge, knowing what and how to measure. How do you know that you are developed physically? How do you know whether or not you are an accomplished musician or artist? Those things have to be measured, and progress must be noted. The same is true for moral development. How do you know if you have reached moral perfection? That is a personal measurement of intangibles, but that assessment or evaluation of those traits must be made.

Moral Obligation/Moral Expectation

Moral obligation or expectation is a certain instinct in each individual, regardless of moral training, that strongly indicates an innate sense of right and wrong. It expresses the reality that we have certain moral obligations to society but also that we have certain moral expectations of others as well. For example, our courts of law expect people to tell the truth under oath. There are penalties when people perjure themselves because the moral expectation or obligation is that the truth will and must be told when legal issues are being considered. If someone takes your wallet or pocketbook, you object to their behavior, regardless of your or their religious orientation. That is because you have a moral expectation of how they will treat your property, and they have a moral obligation to follow that expectation.

Moral Disposition

When I teach my morality and ethics seminars, this area generates more discussion than almost anything else because it's so personal. I ask students to identify historical characters who are honorable or dishonorable. After that discussion, we then discuss what caused each person present in the seminar to go into law enforcement or the military. Moral disposition is an ethical temperament that has been formed by life experiences, which create in individuals the moral standards for right or wrong—it is simply one's internal moral position. It has been formed through hardship and life experiences, and it is what reveals one's basic character. In most cases, those in the seminars had someone who impacted their lives as a role model who caused them to consider law enforcement or the military.

A personal example of this concept is that I was raised to be patriotic. That is why I enlisted in the military twice, at the ages of 17 and 41. My moral disposition is to serve my country, and that is even now being expressed through my seminars and this book. My father was a disabled veteran, and I felt a moral obligation to pay back to my country for the 100% disability support provided for my father.

Moral Habituation or Formation

Don't let the word "habituation" intimidate you. It simply means the forming of one's moral interior by exercise and instruction. We need to be formed and not just informed where moral action is concerned. It is the moral engraving of the soul; the etchings in the moral innards of a person that reveals the true character of that individual moral agent. When I was stationed in Korea, there was one subtle encounter with another woman that made me uneasy. She pursued me one day after hours to thank me for my help, but I left the building by another door rather than face her. You may think that was foolish, but, for me, my moral etching of faithfulness to my wife took over and I avoided any semblance of temptation.

16

Moral Consensus

Moral consensus is when a group of reasonable adults agrees on moral parameters. They do not agree in a democratic fashion, but through the means of group consensus. Most people believe that consensus is total agreement, but that is not the case. Consensus occurs when everyone has a chance to contribute and have their input factored into a moral decision, but the consensus of the correct path becomes evident and everyone agrees to abide by the consensus decision as reasonable moral agents. In other words, this consensus is not by majority rule but rather through the consensus of the group dynamic.

Morally Immature and Mature

Morally immature people are the product of stunted moral growth among those who have not pursued moral development. They can remain morally immature well into their adult years. Morally mature people are those who have developed morally to such an extent that they become examples for others, and may even teach or mentor others. They have reached or are close to their moral potential.

Governing Principles

Governing principles are used by morally-developed people to direct their lives. Values may be imposed by an outside agency or group, but principles are personal, regardless of what others say is proper behavior. They have been instilled internally, so that people are governed by them and not by situational ethics. Self-government is morally superior to rule-keeping and other external ways of controlling the behavior of others. Someone who contributes help to every natural disaster is being guided by a governing principle to help those in need. They do not need to ponder or research, or have someone order them to help; their governing principle of compassion directs their behavior in almost every situation.

Social Dictates

Social dictates are social conventions (the word used here in the sense of customs) that dictate to the individual what is proper and socially acceptable. Propriety and demeanor are the operative words that govern this arena. When someone hands you a business card in Asia, you must receive it with two hands and you must read it immediately, or the giver is offended. In Western culture, the card can be put in a pocket to be read later. In some cultures, a burp after a meal is a compliment; in other cultures, the burp is an offense. It requires that the visitor or the resident be aware of the social dictates and be willing to fit in by obeying those dictates. On one occasion, I was close enough to the Queen of England to touch her, but social dictates forbid me to speak to her unless she addressed me. My American value of egalitarianism was trumped by British protocol with royalty.

Civility

Civility has to do with creating a civilization through social norms and proper behavior. To be civil is to be socially sophisticated. Manners and etiquette are also part of civility. When there is a clash between civilizations, there must be a certain level of awareness in each of the groups so that peace and deference can prevail. In World War II, this cultural awareness was lacking when we saw the clash of civilizations between Japan and the U.S. Japanese soldiers were taught never to surrender to the enemy. When Americans surrendered, the Japanese soldiers were so shocked that the Japanese mistreated the Americans because they considered them cowards, and the Americans could not understand their cruelty. There were other reasons for the mistreatment, but part of it was a clash between two well-developed civilizations with differing values.

Moral Leadership

Moral leadership provides moral direction in complex situations. This is in contrast to other kinds of leadership, such as a professional skill or entrepreneurial inspiration. Moral leadership is usually provided by those who are morally mature and developed, those who have moved beyond being just rule keepers. They have internalized and habituated their convictions and are moved by a moral compass, rather than public opinion. Others look to them for guidance and as role models.

Chivalry

Chivalry is the demeanor and mannerism of the gentle and kind. It is characterized by gallantry and good manners. At times, however, it is simply external and does not reflect the core of the individual. *Mildness* is a word commonly used in moral manuals and books in the context of chivalry. It indicates a strong person who can harness his or her strength in a positive direction. A strong man has the capability to harm a young child or a woman, but chivalry demands that he discipline or harness his potential toward positive ends. This practice is certainly less honored and expected in twenty-first century cultures, but, in the past, chivalry was an important part of being civilized and cultured.

Etiquette

Etiquette is the body of social rules for eating and social interaction with a sophisticated group. One must know the cadence and the protocol (which courses are served in what order, what utensils are to be used, how the food is to be eaten, what greetings are appropriate, etc.), which all convey elegant social manners. Customs and decorum are a must in those situations. This is especially evident at social events that require it, such as a formal military ball. There, rules of etiquette govern dress, greetings, and protocols of who does what and when they do it.

Mores

Mores are socially-accepted customs in any given culture that include taboos to be avoided by everyone in the culture, whether they are citizens or not. The root of the word leads us to moral customs or behaviors that do not greatly differ from one culture to the next. An example of a mores in a Muslim culture is that it is forbidden for a woman to show her face to any man except her husband or close family. Another example is that murder (as opposed to killing) is forbidden in any culture with which I am familiar. The same is true for rape. It is true you cannot legislate righteousness, but you can, and most societies do, legislate morality.

Customs

Customs are traditions held in esteem by national cultures. They are not necessarily rooted in law, but have almost the same authority as the law in the lives of those who observe and are subject to them. The Thanksgiving holiday in the U.S. is a good example. It is celebrated to honor the work of the early American settlers (which at times was at the expense of the Native American residents), but is not recognized by any other culture. In Japan, it is part of the culture that a person bows when he or she meets someone. If you don't bow, they won't throw you out of the country, but it can be socially embarrassing. In the U.S., we shake hands, and both are examples of cultural customs.

Revealed Law

Revealed law is law that has been revealed by other than a divine rather than a human source. Revealed law is reflected in the moral terrain of all mankind. All legitimate law derives from this transcendent source. We will discuss this more in the next chapter.

This moral vocabulary will aid any person who is learning the terrain of moral issues. I have attempted to give brief definitions so that you can refer to and use the moral vocabulary as an aid in your moral understanding, as we move through this book. Words and their meanings are important when one is learning a new language, and morality and moral development are no exceptions. I have compiled the definitions from various sources to help you build on your understanding of morality and virtue.

Before we move on, however, let's talk about morale's effect on community and how it stems from morality. Morale, which is closely related to morality, is the moral effect on a community when its spirit is healthy. When its spirit is not healthy, it is what we characterize as being demoralized. Virginia Tech University experienced a mass shooting on its campus in April 2007, and the entire campus was demoralized by the immorality of one individual. Evil stole the school's spirit for a short time. Only good behavior and civility restored the school's soul as time went on.

Edmund Burke uttered these famous words, "Evil prevails when good men do nothing." Consider also Japan and Germany after World War II. They both had to face the implications of their immoral behaviors, and the people were dispirited and downcast. It took decades to rebuild both nations, as they accumulated years of positive moral actions that overcame their moral lapses. Can you see how morale is tied to morality?

When one is demoralized, the process of regaining a moral position is a rigorous one. During the campus crisis at Virginia Tech, the President of the United States quoted a biblical passage that gave the campus hope when he said, "Do not be overcome with evil but overcome evil with good" (Romans 12:21). The message is that evil can be overcome by good, but it takes effort and intentionality. The proverb has been proven true, since there was an outpouring of good will from almost the entire world to that one hurting community.

Now that we have defined the terms, we are ready to move on with our discussion to prove that moral development is possible and necessary, if we are going to have and regain a just and moral society.

QUESTIONS FOR REFLECTION

1. Why is it important to understand the moral terrain before you begin to travel on it?

2. What aspect of the moral terrain were you unfamiliar with and were introduced to for the first time in your company? A foreign country? Another family?

3. What words were most helpful to you from this list of definitions? Where are you still confused and need to do a bit more study and research?

CHAPTER 3

CAN VIOLENT MEN

BECOME VIRTUOUS?

Most people who are called upon to use force in their line of work are considered by the uninformed as violent men and women because they must use force at times in the line of duty. This misconception is hard to overcome, especially when news reports of seemingly violent activity are widely broadcast. Many of the modern writers I have consulted have been unwilling to distinguish between necessary deadly force and senseless violence. I will attempt to make the distinction clearer than the politically-charged conversation currently being conducted has allowed.

An example that we have seen all too often in modern culture is the random shooter on a rampage, who must be killed in order to preserve innocent life. That is an example of the need for deadly force. When prisoners of war are subjected to humiliation and torture, and photographed in the process, however, we have all beheld an example of senseless violence, and that label can be applied to any and all military personnel engaged in similar activity. To understand the difference, let's clarify the historical distinction in the words *killing* and *murder*.

On the one hand, killing occurs when one is exercising the natural right of self-defense. On the other hand, murder is accompanied by malice. When one is called to be an "agent of the state" in the role of military or police, personal vengeance must be laid aside. The true police or military professional develops the necessary character that keeps this tension between vengeance and protection in check. The image of knowing when to be steel and when to be velvet is helpful when making this determination. Society must ask if it wants passive or cowardly protectors, or those who can recognize the distinction between violence and deadly force. Society should want professionals who have the ability to face evil head on, but can also restrain and harness that strength.

Now, let's begin to address the question that is the title for this chapter: Can violent people become virtuous? The key word in this question is *become*, because moral development is a process, as we have already pointed out. The question arises as to whether or not any of the moral development theories of history have been proven effective. Our examination will start with the life of Socrates. Socrates (469-399 B.C.) was a Greek philosopher who most have heard of, but few know many of the specifics of his life. Socrates was not a writer, but his thoughts and teaching impacted many of his contemporaries, and millions since. Socrates made the point that only an examined life is a life worth living.

Socrates was an example of a person who submitted to a process to become "something." Every process has a starting point and an end point when the process is completed. Moral development is such a process. The starting point, according to Socrates, is self-knowledge. "Know thyself" is the maxim that describes the first stage of this process. Socrates did not say "know *about* thyself," but rather he said, "Know thyself." What did Socrates really mean by this statement?

Self-knowledge starts with the willingness to be self-deprecating. To know one's self deeply requires honesty and humility. An accurate perception of self and the real self are often unattainable, however, because of dishonesty and self-deception. When people tell others, "I am basically an honest person," and then cheat on their taxes, they are not capable of the kind of honesty needed to achieve self-knowledge.

What's more, no person should be defined by the opinions or feedback of others, but anyone can gain insight into himself (or herself) from the input of others. That input from others still requires personal honesty, if the feedback is going to contribute toward moral development. If I confront the tax cheater and say, "You are dishonest," that cheater must accept my assessment or else defend his actions by saying, "No, I'm not, besides everyone does it." That response will prevent moral development because there is denial that any problem exists in the first place.

When people truly know themselves, they know their failures and limitations as well as their potential. For example, people I referenced above who have cheated on their taxes should be thinking, "I have cheated before, so I will turn my tax preparation over to a professional." By doing so, they are not putting themselves in a situation that could result in a moral failure. Every morally developing person should know his or her limitations before ever stepping into a situation—and recognize his or her need for input from others.

When you don't know yourself, you will trust yourself in certain situations more than you should. "I can handle it" is a denial that one has any such limitations. A great and courageous King David in the Old Testament once said, "I don't involve myself in things too difficult for me." There are certain areas that one should protect oneself from by not accepting assignments that would expose them to being vulnerable, and by being honest with co-workers and superiors. This honesty, however, must begin with self-awareness and self-knowledge.

Recently, I heard of a well-respected child psychologist who had to excuse himself from a pornography review board initiated by the government because of the intensity of the subject matter. He did not believe he could be objective, based on what he knew about the case, so rather than err in judgment, he excused himself from the process. It can be humbling to admit one's vulnerability, but it is better to deal with it in a proactive way than by having a moral failure that tarnishes or even ruins a career—or one of another person.

Let me provide another example of personal honesty from a popular movie to further illustrate what I am talking about. In the first *Star Wars* episode, Yoda is training Luke Skywalker, who believes he is ready to face the evil lord, Darth Vader. At one point early in his training, Luke has a sense to go into a cave, and Yoda does not prevent him, even though Yoda has been warning Luke that he is not ready to face Vader.

Luke proceeds into the cave and, sure enough, there is Darth Vader. They engage in combat and Luke is able to decapitate Vader. When the head rolls to Luke's feet, however, the mask comes down and lo and behold, Luke sees his face behind the mask. The point of that vision is that Luke had not faced the reality of who he was or his moral limitations. He had a dark side in him just like was in Darth Vader, and he was capable of doing what Vader had done earlier in his career.

Luke's denial and zeal to put himself in a situation for which he was not prepared almost cost him and many others their lives. Luke had the valor, but Yoda knew that he did not have the virtue. He was willing to be violent for a cause, but he had not developed morally in order to become a true Jedi warrior. That development had to include an accurate self-assessment of who Luke truly was and what he was capable of doing in addition to his Jedi light sabre training.

In almost any other field except where valor is a premium, professionals can readily acknowledge their weaknesses. For instance, strength tests for fire personnel reveal this reality. If we are weightlifting together and it is your turn, you will put the amount of weight on the bar that you can handle. If I can lift more than you, you should not say, "I can handle that, too" and proceed to lift. That would not be smart, and prove to be harmful to your physical well-being. If in the physical realm, our limitations are clear and easy to confess, why is it not the same for our moral capabilities?

The answer to the question will be answered with another question, in the teaching style of Socrates: How can I measure my moral capacity? Or how can I grow in my moral capacity? When one gets into an elevator, there is usually a sign that reads, "Capacity 2,000 pounds." If there are ten people on the elevator and they all weigh about 200 pounds, the elevator is almost at capacity. If someone is lying about or unaware of their weight, the other nine people may be in trouble!

Moral capacity, however, is not fixed like physical capacity. It is in an entirely different realm with a different measurement. Moral capacity is measured by the ability or inability to act morally! That capacity may not be revealed until you face a situation that requires virtue! As I write, there are some Olympic athletes who were caught in a compromising situation, and then lied and stated that they were robbed, when they had actually committed a crime of vandalism. Their moral capacity was revealed to be small and their need to develop was great.

The good news to our question is that all men and women *can* become virtuous, even if they must be violent in carrying out their duties. Every reasonable person is, at the starting point, a moral equal; however, the ultimate goal and capacity for each person is determined by the individual and the price he or she is willing to pay to develop that moral potential. We will talk about a strategy of how to grow and increase moral capacity later in this book. Before we get there, however, I need to prove the possibility of internalizing virtue. I am not convinced that you are yet a "believer." More work has to be done!

Potential is an important consideration in this study of virtue. Endowments and natural gifts need also to be evaluated, for some seem to have a more sensitive conscience than others. Limitations or growth boundaries that you place on yourself, however, can sometimes limit you from reaching your full potential, no matter what your natural inclination may be. You must understand where you are now, so that you can reach your desired goal in the future.

Let's return to the weight-lifting analogy for a moment. There are some people who can lift more than others, all things being equal, even though they have not trained to lift. If you can lift 185 pounds, but your goal is to lift 200 pounds, you must work up to being able to lift 15 more pounds. If your starting capacity is 150 pounds, you will have to work harder and longer to get to the 200-pound goal. Both must exercise and train their muscles, but the one has to work a bit more. Every long-distance runner also knows this routine and reality.

In the moral realm, you must also exercise and practice a moral habit in order for it to be formed correctly, and you must start from where you are. Most habits take at least 21 days to be established, according to some experts in the field. For some, it may take a bit longer. We, as a culture, have not followed this rule, so we use the excuse that something is not attainable, instead of exerting more effort to make it happen. Mankind has progressed considerably in all known realms *except* in the moral realm.

The question we should be asking before we move on is this: How much does predisposition have to do with our ability to choose? In considering moral capacity, why can some lift 185 pounds while other can only lift 150? Is the lifter of 150 pounds relegated to that weight limit for the remainder of his or her life? If we cannot choose to improve morally because of the circumstances that have formed us or predisposed us to be or act a certain way, then how can we exercise our free will to form new, positive habits? If we cannot choose and we are predisposed to be weak or even evil, then what hope is there? Not much. My premise is that anyone can increase the moral weight they lift, just like the example of the lifters who start at different capabilities.

The question of free will has been discussed for centuries. The basic question is: Is it truly free and how free is it? As moral agents, humans must take responsibility for their actions by accepting that free will is definitely free. The excuse that you did not know better or that your environment took away your ability to choose does not square with moral history or with the concept of universals.

If you remember, a universal is a moral concept that exists in all cultures, one such as "taking another life is wrong." There are too many cultures that adhere to consistent norms and moral expectations regardless of their environments to deny the existence of those moral norms, as stated in The Universal Declaration of Human Rights published by the United Nations in 1948. More facts will be presented later on in this study and specific examples will be cited where moral universals are concerned. I would recommend C. S. Lewis' book, *The Abolition of Man*, as an excellent study of the universal moral code that exists across all cultures. Lewis' research substantiates the concept that there is a universal moral code maintained by most societies.

We have been asking the question: "Can a person develop morally, regardless of that person's predisposition?" Instead of that question, perhaps we should be asking: "Do humans *want* to develop morally?" Willpower is a major factor in the process of moral development, and this, too, can be exercised and enhanced. Exercising your will makes it stronger and forms a habit of doing so! Developing resistance against evil inclinations takes time and patience. It is a weak excuse to say that you do not have the moral power to resist evil. The defining question is: Do you really *want* to resist it? If someone is weak-willed, the only reason is because they have not exercised their will.

Why should one resist evil? There is a profound saying in the Bible that goes like this: "Don't be overcome by evil, but instead overcome evil with good" (Romans 12:21). This statement doesn't make sense if you are under the impression that evil is irresistible and more powerful than good. Perhaps evil is not more powerful, and it is only a false perception. Yet a false perception can be a reality where the holder of the perception is concerned. Why does it seem easier to follow the herd? The herd mentality is a sociological concept that seems to border on fatalism, in essence denying the power of human individuality and free will. Flip Wilson, a comedian, used a comedy routine in which he claimed, "The devil made me do it!" That is an example of fatalism where morality is concerned.

Let's return to the question that is the underlying one for this chapter and, in a sense, for the entire book: "Can the violent become virtuous?" The answer is a hardy, "Yes they can!" Now that we have established this truth, what can we do about it?

Sir Lancelot (one of the knights of the Round Table under King Arthur), a brave and competent character, faced the question we are examining. He was a capable man who had some moral problems due to an underdeveloped character. He was a chivalrous warrior with many gentlemanly (professional) qualities, but had not been totally formed morally. Sir Lancelot was brave, to be sure, but he was not always virtuous! Does his valor or that of any other professional excuse them from the standard that they impose and enforce on others about right and wrong, justice and injustice? Certainly not!

Natural ability, attractiveness, and giftedness (a combination referred to as charisma) sometimes cause the American culture to overlook flaws in a person's character. Sir Lancelot was handsome and to some as beautiful as a "god," which at times excused his moral failure in the eyes of many. His popularity outweighed the good judgment of those around him because his "beauty" mesmerized them. Why does this charisma negate the need for him and others to be engaged in the development of character? The short answer is that it does not. Lancelot transformed from a heroic to a tragic figure because he did not develop morally, even though he was a mighty warrior to the end.

We all admire heroes and at times secretly dream of being one. Myths and stories like Zorro, King Arthur and his knights, Robin Hood, and Sir Galahad all speak to this need and desire of being heroic. The real question we should ask when we consider these heroes is: "Were these men in these myths good men or did they just perform good deeds?" Jesus made an interesting comment regarding this enigma. He said, "You being evil give good gifts to your children" (Matthew 7:11), which basically means our essence is evil but we are still capable of doing good things. When a person does good even though that person is evil, that does not mean the person is good, but it does indicate they are capable of doing good!

There is a distinction here in the same way that there is a distinction in the words of Socrates, which described the concept of "know thyself." Socrates did not say (as stated before) know *about* thyself. Instead, he declared that you are to know who you *truly* are, and that is where "goodness" begins! Your actions do not always define or reveal your essence. Your essence is the real you, and eventually your actions will always reveal that reality even if, at times, you choose to act differently.

Your *consistent* actions do indeed define the real you because they are a sign of maturity and an indication you have acquired virtue (or not). This conclusion is in line with traditional Aristotelian theory. The consistency (or habit) is what forms your essence. Habit forms character (good or bad). You must internalize your beliefs in order to form good qualities so you can perform moral deeds.

Formation instead of information alone will help you create a character that will enable a person of dignity (who possesses royal character) to embrace the sacred trust that is required in a vocation such as law enforcement or the military (where bravery is necessary), It will also bestow the role of overseeing moral accountability to the community that has entrusted the protectors of society with such an honor!

What is a hero? Is a hero something someone *does* or is it something someone *is*? For instance, consider the fire personnel involved in the World Trade Center terrorist attack. Were they heroes that day alone or were they heroes when they decided to serve humankind by becoming fire personnel? When did they decide to save lives: on September 11th or on the day that they signed on the dotted line to join the force? You can answer that question for yourself. The truth remains, then that the violent (rugged, brave, tough) *can* become virtuous *after* they have finished with the process of moral development.

QUESTIONS FOR REFLECTION

1. Is *violent* an appropriate term for those who have demonstrated valor? If not, why not? What would you choose as an alternative descriptor?

2. Do you believe every person has the capability of growing morally? Do you agree that it is a matter of the will and not a matter of some internal predisposition?

3. What or who are some of the sources in your life that have contributed to your moral development?

CHAPTER 4

WHY VALOR

IS NOT ENOUGH

Sometimes, those who are perceived to be brave get a pass from much of society, when it comes to issues of morality. Like Sir Lancelot, many of the brave are young and handsome, and represent the hope of the future. Their charm and helpfulness often exempt them from the greater responsibility of moral formation, especially in the military. They look good but the question is: Are they really good? Do they have to be good in order to be great? This is a question that we will examine in this chapter.

When someone is called a good man or woman, does the description pertain to that person's deeds or to the essence of their character? Can a good person do evil deeds? Can an evil person do good deeds? As stated earlier, the theory that moral formation is possible is demonstrable. Repetition is the key to moral internalization. Moral theory cannot create moral fortitude until it is practiced. A baseball player who does not practice hitting will lose his edge. As a runner, when I lay off for a few days, I lose momentum and endurance. Practice, more practice, and repetition are the keys to my success as a runner. They are the same keys to moral development and success.

Let's look at the statement that is the title for this chapter:

Why valor is not enough. Allow me, if you will, to build a scenario. Most people are impressed with kindness and bravery. These are the external appearances of a chivalrous person. When we remove their armor and get past their sweet talk, we may have a dangerous person on our hands, if that person is not moral. The appearance of virtue in that case is a great deception, for both the holder and the beholder. The danger is more severe for persons who think they are what they appear to be more than for the other person believing the lie. The concept of self-deception is actually more dangerous than deliberate or intentional deception of others.

The difference between image and substance is the issue in this scenario. Let me use a somewhat crude illustration to demonstrate my point. Upon completion of answering nature's call, one should wash his or her hands. If you step up to the soap dispenser, however, and it is beautiful or functional but has no soap in it, it cannot fulfill its purpose. It appears to be something that it is not. It is a cloud without water, a biblical example found in Jude 1:12. The dispenser has image, but no real substance.

Those of us who have worn our nation's military uniforms know this trap, especially if we have several medals, ribbons, and other awards and achievements to show from our service time. I have worn two military uniforms—the U.S. Navy during the Vietnam War and the U.S. Army up until 2005. I was an enlisted man, as well as an officer. I appeared to be something that many times I was not. Upon receiving my active duty interview at West Point—the U.S. Military Academy—the military interviewer asked me not to wear my uniform so that he would not be mesmerized by my military accomplishments, but instead get to the heart of the matter—my character!

This truth was and is apparent to everyone except for the person projecting the image. Take off the shell (the uniform) and what do you have? This is the question for which we must all seek an honest answer. Is image enough or do I need to have the moral goods? Some of our public officials have told us that the public self and the private self are totally different entities. In ethical terms, this is called duplicity. Integrity, on the other hand, is when a person has integrated both sides of his or her life (public and private) to be a consistently whole person. In a good sense, we say about that person, "What you see is what you get." There are no moral surprises.

Conscience is a topic we have briefly talked about that should be addressed more fully at this juncture. Does everyone have a conscience? It seems that all do, but a conscience must be formed and informed. What about the function of blushing that was mentioned earlier? Is that related to the conscience? I propose that blushing is an indicator of the sensitivity of the conscience expressed physically through an increase of blood rushing to the face. Why is blushing so important? For the same reason that the oil light on your dashboard is important. It is a warning signal that, if ignored, could result in a ruined engine that will destroy the functionality of the car. The conscience serves the same purpose.

The Old Testament prophet Jeremiah twice referred to the inability to blush as an indicator of moral decline and failure. The first verse is found in Jeremiah 6:15: "'Are they ashamed of their detestable conduct? No, they have no shame at all; they do not even know how to blush. So they will fall among the fallen; they will be brought down when I punish them,' says the LORD." The other verse is found in Jeremiah 8:12 and says, "Are they ashamed of their detestable conduct? No, they have no shame at all; they do not even know how to blush. So they will fall among the fallen; they will be brought down when they are punished, says the Lord."

I knew a young lady once, who was a counselor. When she went to college, she was quite concerned because she lost the ability to blush. After she settled down, got married, and became a counselor, she was relieved that she could blush again. Her regular exposure to things that at one time would have embarrassed her had actually de-sensitized her to the reality that those things were morally dubious.

Indications, like a tinge of conscience, reveal the state and level of our moral development. Alexander the Great (a student of Aristotle) was said to be extremely handsome, brave, and a natural leader. He was a military commander with extraordinary gifts. He died at the age of 33, however, due to his immoral lifestyle and lack of moral development. He divided his kingdom among his closest associates, but they were unable to maintain what Alexander had built and the world was plunged into chaos for centuries after his death.

Perhaps it would be helpful to look at the studies of moral development made famous by Lawrence Kohlberg and further explained by his "student," George Sher. Lawrence Kohlberg (born 1927) was professor of educational and social psychology at Harvard University. According to these men, the process of moral development goes as follows:

Preconventional Level – "At this level, the child is responsive to cultural rules and labels of good and bad, right or wrong, but interprets these labels in terms of either the physical or the hedonistic consequences of action (punishment, reward, exchange of favors) or in terms of the physical power of those who enunciate the rules..."

Conventional Level – "At this level, maintaining the expectations of the individual's family, group, or nation is perceived as valuable in its own right, regardless of immediate and obvious consequences."

Principled Level – "At this level, there is clear effort to define moral values and principles that have validity and application apart from the authority of the groups or people holding these principles" (Kohlberg, 1971).

These levels of maturity can only be realized and achieved as people become cognizant of their progress through each one.

Progress can only be made when each level is embraced and thoroughly completed. There are no shortcuts to the process. Not everyone agrees with Kohlberg's assessment of this process, however. I do not reject the Kohlberg tradition, but would say that it is incomplete. It characterizes the problem but does not give a lasting solution.

Virtue ethics and character development provide a core that is consistent for any person who experiences real change and transformation. Those internal changes are not just external conformity to a moral code. The summaries of the three levels above are helpful in that they enable individuals to identify where they are in the process of moral development, but are deficient in that they have no power to direct them through the process. In other words, if I step on a scale and see that I am 165 pounds, I know exactly where I am. The problem is that the scale cannot tell me how to reach 145 or 185. That's the same problem with Kohlberg's levels. They tell us where we are but are of no help to tell us how to move on.

Dr. Donald Demarco, under the rubric of integrity, discusses a concept referred to as "multiplicity" when he wrote, "Multiplicity is fragmentation, fractionalization, dispersion, and dividedness" (Demarco, 2000). In other words, when someone appears to be one person externally, but is really another internally, they are going off in different directions at the same time! Dr. Demarco suggests that the opposite of multiplicity is integrity, which is wholeness and unity.

Becoming a whole person, rather than fragments and compartments, is the goal of moral development at the third level or stage of Kohlberg's development. To say that one has a private life and a public life is to deny the need for integration. A mature person must be consistent in his or her behavior, whether public or private, whether someone is watching or not. True integrity is revealed in the predictability of a virtuous person's behavior. This behind-the-scenes development process is unseen to the naked eye until it is demonstrated through a consistent lifestyle. Aristotle put it this way: "Pleasure in doing virtuous acts is a sign that the virtuous disposition has been acquired."

This unity has to do with the fragments of a person's character all moving in the same direction to accomplish a common task. Let's use an example from the old South during Jim Crow days. The law enforcement had the appearance of upholding the law, but, at night, some of those officials were Ku Klux Klan terrorists and sympathizers! That is a perfect example of multiplicity, and some would call it duplicity. Integrity would have been practiced and evidenced if those officers would have protected the rights of *all* people and not just of the white majority.

QUESTIONS FOR REFLECTION

1. Why is duplicity (having a private persona and a public persona) dangerous to moral development?

2. Why is integration of these dispositions a true indication of integrity?

3. What does the word integrity mean to you? How do you apply it in your life, professionally and personally?

CHAPTER 5

MORE ON MORAL

DEVELOPMENT

This behind-the-scenes development process is unseen to the naked eye until it is demonstrated through a consistent life-style. Aristotle put it this way: "Pleasure in doing virtuous acts is a sign that the virtuous disposition has been acquired." In other words, when you enjoy integrity because it is the right thing to you, you are well on your way in your moral development.

Moral formation is the starting point and process that leads to moral development. As stated earlier, natural ability and giftedness sometimes cause American culture to overlook flaws in character. This process of moral formation will eliminate this often dangerous and confusing practice of externalism—putting more weight in how things look than how they are. Because habit forms character (good or bad), one must internalize one's values in order to form good dispositions. We are not desirous of individuals who are only good on the outside (externalism), but who are also good in the core of their being (internalism).

Qualities of character work in degrees. For instance, in truth telling, the degree of veracity that one possesses depends on the formation of this character. Is it *consistent* or is it *convenient*? Do I *live* the truth or do I only occasionally *tell* the truth? This consistency, or lack thereof, determines character development at its highest degree. It takes practice and consistency to become good at it. It is a process that will more than likely take a lifetime.

Humans are not naturally truthtellers. Are you surprised by that assessment? Those with children will be less surprised at this assumption. This is why we must work so diligently at the process of developing virtue. Exaggeration functions in children more readily than it does in adults, but a white lie is still a lie! Lying reveals that veracity and integrity are still deficient in the individual. In developing morally, one does not always get it right. The more consistent one becomes, the more developed he or she is becoming. As Aristotle said, when it is done with joy, one has arrived at a level of maturity and has acquired a degree of the virtuous life.

Are you beginning to see how shortsighted valor is without the element of virtue present? Years ago, there was movie by the name, *And Justice for All*, starring Al Pacino. There was a line in the movie that has haunted me for years. When it was discovered that the judge was crooked, Al Pacino, upon leaving the courtroom (I believe he was being forcibly removed), shouted to the judge, "You are supposed to stand for something." I was deeply moved by these words. The image is that a judge stands for justice, but when he or she perverts justice, that person makes a mockery of their position.

No one is perfect (that is the standard, however), but the striving must never stop until it is accomplished. Can one have a perfect score in bowling? Can people improve their game of golf? Can one break a record in track that fifty years ago no one ever thought possible? These are achievable goals, which can be attained. Moral development works the same way. You will hit plateaus and then press through to the next level.

Most Americans do not believe that moral development is possible. We have bought into the lie that "I am *only* human." We sell ourselves short with this mentality, for our moral potential is great! If we are lazy, then it is easier to live with the philosophy that people cannot be any better. For real "men" and "women," there is a more challenging journey that will produce lasting results! There will be dragons to fight and fleshly appetites to overcome, but no one can help others until they have overcome themselves, literally and figuratively.

Men of valor who lack virtue are incomplete heroes. To prove this point, I want to tell you a story about two kings. William Shakespeare describes one for us; and the other one is King David from the Bible. On the one hand, Shakespeare writes in *King Henry VI, Part One*, "England ne'er had a king until his time. Virtue he had, deserving to Command." David, on the other hand, did not cease to be king when he committed adultery, but it certainly impeded his effectiveness. David was a man of valor devoid of character, which is the essence of virtue. King Henry, according to Shakespeare, was a true king, the first in fact, because he had virtue.

How do we distinguish between form and substance where virtue is concerned? Is it image that looks good, as opposed to substance, that measures the essence of a man? What *looks* good and what *is* good? Does the outer shell of a man necessarily reveal his substance? These questions and more must be addressed if we are to go any further in this study.

Does virtue qualify us or disqualify us to lead? A famous Civil War General was quoted as saying, "I will never put someone into command who cannot command himself." General Robert E. Lee himself was a model of such discipline and restraint, and proved that character does count in military leadership! General H. Norman Swartzkoff, now deceased, said once, "To be a twenty-first-century leader, you must have two things: competence and character."

We put such a stress on competence that we sometimes forget character. Then, what happens in the long run is that our lack of character will be a stumbling block to advancement—it will sabotage our progress. Virtue is what a man *is*; valor is what a man *does*. Let me share with you several characteristics that I have discovered in many great soldiers and great men and women:

1. They were patriotic; they went to war for their countries.

2. They were scholars, some even soldier-scholars.

3. Many of them became statesmen as a result of those two traits.

4. Many of them were religious men and women as well.

These components are important factors in professional development, as are the suggestions of General Schwartzkopf. A consummate professional is not just proficient in his or her work, but also has the character to go with it. This has often been the missing link in true professionalism. We admire the skilled person above the honest person. We give our awards and medals based on what people have done, not according to who they are (the exception being the good conduct medal). We therefore get what we honor, so when we honor valor, we only get more valor. When we starve goodness, it becomes less and less prevalent.

While I was a solider at Fort Bragg, I saw awards given for technical proficiency but never for honesty. Skill is important, but a skillful person without integrity is an accident waiting to happen. Consider the mythical scientist Victor Frankenstein. He had knowledge, but not the moral parameters and confinements to work within any moral restraints, and he created a monster. Knowledge without morality is dangerous. The one informs the other and the one is incomplete without the other. For another example, look at Einstein's comment on religion and science:

1. For the scientific method can teach us nothing else beyond how facts are related to, and conditioned by, each other. The aspiration toward such objective knowledge belongs to the highest of

which man is capable, and you will certainly not suspect me of wishing to belittle the achievements and the heroic efforts of man in this sphere. Yet it is equally clear that knowledge of what is does not open the door directly to what *should be* (Einstein, 1939).

His quote is insightful and helpful in understanding the necessary balance when deliberating about faith and reason. People who possess the knowledge that their character cannot handle will eventually do great injustice to the world around them. Take for instance nuclear weaponry. If put into the hands of people who lack character and good will, this would threaten the safety of the whole world.

Character also counts, especially when secrets about national security are at stake. There are too many examples in our nation's history regarding espionage to ignore this point. Character formation must start in childhood because of the inclination and proclivity of waywardness. Now if this process has not started in childhood, it is more difficult to begin, but not impossible to achieve, during adulthood.

Many outstanding leaders in history started this process later in life, and Ignatius of Loyola is a good example to prove this point. Ignatius lived in the sixteenth century and was a soldier. He was not a religious or virtuous man; in fact, he was the opposite. After a serious injury, however, he came to his senses. His moral development program, or as he called it, "spiritual exercises," was a rigorous plan that led to permanent change.

Working a plan for the process of moral development is certainly a lot more difficult than simply talking about the process. Moral development is a process that requires hard work. Certain endowments, talents, and gifts do not usually require much work, except for a little cultivation. I used weightlifting as an example earlier. Intelligence or intellectual capacity is something that involves comprehension, which requires some effort.

The realm of moral development or ethical training, however, is misunderstood and, consequently, our culture has produced moral deficient individuals and organizations! We have not exerted the energy to develop, and thus, we have atrophied.

Moral development must be built up and acquired in the same way any other component of our being is cultivated. Due to the fact that this realm of moral development is "invisible," quantifying the results is not always easy, but this does not mean that the results are not demonstrable. Character is contagious; bad habits, as well as good ones, are imparted partly by association. The impartation, however, is just the beginning of the process. The association must be accompanied by consistent application for at least twenty-one days.

For example, if I want to form a habit of getting up at 4 a.m. every morning, I must do it consistently for three weeks before it is formed as a part of my character. This process also works with telling the truth. It is not enough to only stop lying. I must replace that bad habit by consistently telling the truth. This process, which has been compared to swimming in peanut butter, as stated earlier, is grueling.

Professionals who, as part of their work, embrace discipline will welcome this grueling process. The question in this chapter has been; "Why is valor not enough?" It is like having a roller coaster without the tracks, a beach without the sand, and a honeycomb without the honey. We will now turn our attention to learn how to speak the language of morality.

QUESTIONS FOR REFLECTION:

1. Do you agree that valor is not enough? What situations will not be overcome by valor alone?

2. Are you willing to make the effort to develop morally, or is it enough to talk about it?

3. Do you really think it's a problem to live one life professionally and another life personally?

CHAPTER 6

WILL REAL MEN PAY

THE PRICE FOR VIRTUE?

All that has been discussed, so far, about a moral escalation in civilized society cannot happen without a commitment from real men and strong women. Those who are tired of sitting back, feeling helpless in the face of active evil, must take action now. American culture has become almost fatalistic in the face of current events. We don't really believe that the moral tide can turn towards the good.

The word *sacrifice* has lost its meaning in American culture due to this moral passivity. What will it take to devise a plan that will renew America from the inside out? This plan must have more to do with America being *good* than it does with America being *great*. In times past, our distinguished country had more of a reputation for goodness than it did for greatness. Now, it seems that we have reversed the two and have sold our identity for riches.

Before we continue, let's ask ourselves what we want America to look like one hundred years from now. This will be determined by our action or inaction today. The truth of the matter is that there are internal realities that exist in each of us (natural law that indicates things are not right as they should be), and that means we cannot help but get socially involved. If this social action is self-absorbed and hedonistic, we send a message that we really don't care about the world around us or future generations, unless it personally affects and benefits us.

As each tragedy occurs in America, it seems disaster comes closer to our homes every day. Will this call us as a nation to action or will we dull our senses by our indulgence and selfishness? Will our latent virtue only emerge during national crisis? Think of how America was after the tragedy of 9-11. Churches were filled, people were praying, and people were talking to one another. Thousands of people wanted to go to New York to do *something*, and many did. They applauded the first responders, brought them food, and gave them water. Friends reported to me that taxi cabs stopped honking their horns for months after 9-11. Tourists flocked to see the devastation, waiting in long lines and weeping as they observed the horror of the site. My question is: Why can't America be like that all the time? I believe it can.

Because some don't believe this can happen, they speak of a spiritual revival that must come from outside of America. They believe only God can stir up this spirit of morality, similar to events in our past that were called the Great Awakenings. During two Awakenings, citizens experienced tremendous and noticeable spiritual revival. It does not seem that those revivals were tied to anything the citizenry did. They were sovereign acts of God.

I do not deny the occurrence of those Great Awakenings, and I would pray that those phenomena would repeat themselves in our culture. I do not believe, however, that they are necessary in order for what I am presenting in this book to happen. America can "wake up" and begin to pursue new values that pertain to standards of morality and goodness that are universally considered to be good. We simply must believe that it is possible. Many today have abandoned such hope.

Perhaps if we took seriously this tendency to heroism and chivalry as a nation, we could avert some of these national tragedies. It is certainly in our DNA to do so, for historically our nation has risen to the challenge of defending others on several historic occasions. Americans freed Europe and the Pacific, with the help of its Allies, during World War II. We also liberated Kuwait when Saddam Hussein invaded that country. In recent decades, however, we seem to have lost our sense of community, so therefore we have been unable to live up to our national legacy and identity.

Nobility, which was once esteemed in our society, is now looked down upon by many as a wasted effort. There are present-day heroes in American society, no doubt, but collectively we have, to a large extent, lost the desire to stand up for what is right. We fear evil and do not want to counteract it with good. What are we trying to protect? What are we willing to die for? Is anything worth fighting for? What makes a people give up its desire to defend its glorious nation? These and others are important questions for us to ask and answer.

In heroic history and in the discipline of heroic ethics, some live and some die. Some die so that others can live, and then the living have a sacred trust to maintain that legacy to honor the dead and for those yet to be born. History is both linear and cyclical, however, and we must pay attention to its cycles, so that we are not bound to repeat them because of inattention and inactivity. Words like predetermination and predestination leave little room for moral responsibility, for we then believe that our actions will have little if any consequence, and we allow evil to prevail unchallenged.

If we think that everything is fixed and cannot be impacted by people's free will, we will become passive and apathetic in the face of evil. If everything is predetermined, why should mankind even pray, if everything is already predetermined in the mind of God?

When 9-11 occurred, someone fatalistically said to me "Whatever will be, will be." In my estimation, that takes us off the hook of recognizing our responsibility and potential to make things better. With a predetermined mindset that says things are predestined to happen, it causes us to be passive in the face of evil. There is a saying that goes something like this: "Why polish the brass on a sinking ship?" If we think culture is sinking, then we will accept what happens with little thought that it could be avoided or improved.

I do not deny that God has a great master plan for the earth, but I do not accept that free will is limited, or that the individual is not responsible for his or her actions. Someone once said that God is playing chess with man and matches his every move. We can pray and God can say no, for He is the Almighty. But murder is not God's will; that is our invention that stems from our tendency toward evil. St. Augustine stated that if man doesn't have free will, then God cannot judge anyone. We have played a role in the problem, and we can have a role in the solution.

Circumstances and the environment in which we are raised do help shape us to a certain extent, but they do not predetermine or predestine us against our wills. We have many examples of people who have succeeded against all kinds of odds, yet we deny the possibility that this can happen morally. I was raised in the Newark projects with a family that had its share of problems and tragedies. No one in my family went to college, but I was determined, by God's grace, to make the most of the opportunities I had. People who are told to give up their goods or be shot to death don't have much of a choice, but they still have a choice. Socrates, the philosopher, is a prime example of this truth. He chose death to keep his integrity rather than have life and compromise what he taught and believed.

Did Socrates exercise free will, or was he predetermined to meet such a demise? Is it not an empty excuse to refuse to see that humans are moral agents with the freedom to choose? What choice will American culture make when it comes to virtuous men and women? Will we continue to believe that the rite of passage for men in particular is engrossed in immorality and lawlessness?

Let me address men for the moment, who still comprise the majority of leadership in law enforcement and the military. Please, ladies, bear with me, and read with a view toward your own ability to lead and be morally strong. What's more, I am a man and I know what I have faced in my own journey in the military and as an instructor of those in the police world. So, let me speak as a man to men.

Let's ask another difficult question: "Is it harder to be good or to be bad?" The consequences of bad may be harder, but because of our human proclivity toward evil, it's harder to do good! The herd mentality says: "Go with the flow, follow the herd, and follow the crowd." True manhood has the courage to stand alone, like the lion hearts they truly are, and want to be. Why does the United States Marine Corps call for a "few good men"? Have you ever asked yourself that question? Why not a few tough men or a few hard-hitting men or a few sharp-shooting men? Why emphasize goodness, selectivity, and exclusivity? They do that because a good man is hard to find. A hard-working man is easier to find but an honest man can be hard to find. Sports-minded men are easy to find, but a man of integrity can be hard to find. A man with a lot of "toys" is easy to find because the American value of success has more to do with things than with substance or character.

This is an unfortunate development that has taken place in the last fifty years. A man's word was his bond in years gone by; nowadays, a written statement is not even a trustworthy document. Lawyers too often excuse our lack of veracity and simply call it a loophole. Why am I saying all of this? First, it's to challenge men to be willing to pay the price by initially fighting evil in their own lives, and then, in the lives of their families, and subsequently, in their communities and nation.

What will it cost to restore sanity to American society?

What are we willing to pay? The reality is that we will either pay now or pay later, but we will pay either way in the end. What are we willing to pay on the installment plan now that will pay positive dividends later as well?

QUESTIONS FOR REFLECTION

1. Are passivity and apathy the reasons why people of goodwill have not taken action during the crisis that is taking place in America?

2. What responsibility does the male gender have for the condition of American society, due to the fact that they have been in positions of authority for most of the 20th century?

3. What legacy will we leave our children if we give in to the evildoers and let lawlessness prevail?

CHAPTER 7

WHAT IS TRUE?

Let's pretend that we are going for a nice summer ride on a sailboat. The scenery is breathtaking and the water is calm. The sea looks like a mirror and when you stare at it, it mesmerizes you, almost putting you to sleep. All of a sudden a man jumps up and announces he wants to drill a hole under his own seat. He doesn't understand why others should be concerned because it is under his own seat! Several men jump up to resist the man and plug the hole but the man with the drill fights them off. Then, someone on the boat starts to defend the personal rights of the man with the drill. That causes those who were willing to fight the man to sit down and reconsider their position. As they are deliberating, the boat is slowly sinking.

This is what is happening in contemporary society; people have become immobilized due to the opinions of the few. Have men exchanged their instinct to act during danger, for the illogical rhetoric of the foolhardy? Unfortunately, this seems to be the case. Mobilization requires leadership that is proactive and, to some extent, fearless. These leaders are risk takers who are concerned about others, including their children and grandchildren, and not just concerned about their personal comfort for the present. Apathy and the belief that others will get involved or that someone else will do it all keep society at a mediocre moral level.

I am not asking anyone to do more than their natural

talents can support. Not everyone can be a Mother Teresa, but everyone can treat their office petty cash with integrity and not pilfer. Not everyone can be a Dr. Martin Luther King Jr. but some can coach little league or youth volleyball. There are some of you who will lead in places of significance, and others who will raise a family to be courageous and moral. If we all do what we can do, that will be enough.

Sacrifice is a practice that American culture in the twenty-first century tries to avoid. This has not always been the case. Americans made great personal sacrifices during World War II. What has happened to the American spirit that was willing to sacrifice? Who will pay the price to see morality triumph once again? Will it be the children of the next generation because of our unwillingness to sacrifice now? What is the price that must be paid? What price can you pay? It is no more or less than your very life, which again may be faithful service with integrity to your community and position!

Let us quantify what it means to give your life for a cause. The peace-at-any-cost mentality is not the mode of thinking that will bring about lasting results. Appeasing the person who refuses to assimilate into a virtuous society is an indication of a lack of respect for that system. One can disagree on theological grounds but not on the grounds of courtesy and the basic concepts of right and wrong. For example, Muslims can still hold their religious views, but if they refuse to assimilate any of the values of American culture, there will be a problem.

There are community standards to which all recipients must adhere. This is not an imposition of religion but simply of community values. When these standards are deliberately violated, men of virtue must take action! It may inconvenience the *virtue warrior and maybe even cost that person his or her life*; however, somebody has to be willing to pay the price. We must defend the fact that truth is objective and absolute and not just a matter of personal opinion.

At the time of this writing, there have been several violent acts in France. Many immigrants have entered France and were not comfortable with what they experienced in the dominant culture. Therefore, they have exercised their free will and taken matters into their own hands to make a statement through violence and mass killing. At the same time, the French culture has tried to outlaw some Muslim customs like head coverings for women. There must be a middle ground where citizens can maintain their values, but then those citizens must recognize that they have a responsibility to assimilate to some extent into the main culture. They must exert free will to accept that there is a dominant culture and realize that no one can try to impose vigilante justice while maintaining their cultural identity within the dominant culture.

Gangs that are destructive need to be replaced by groups of people committed to moral restoration. The Hell's Angels, the motorcycle gang, wanted to create a nation within a nation. That is counterproductive to morals and virtue and the objectivity of truth. To clarify, let's enter into an ancient conversation that will perhaps help illustrate this point regarding the objectivity of truth.

Protagoras: Truth is relative; it is only a matter of opinion.

Socrates: You mean that truth is mere subjective opinion?

Protagoras: Exactly. What is true for you is true for you, and what is true for me, is true for me. Truth is subjective.

Socrates: Do you really mean that? That my opinion is true by virtue of it being my opinion?

Protagoras: Indeed, I do.

Socrates: My opinion is: Truth is absolute, not opinion, and that you, Mr. Protagoras, are absolutely in error. Since this is my opinion, then you must grant that it is true according to your philosophy.

Protagoras: You are quite correct, Socrates.

If someone said that milk is white and another says milk

is black, both cannot be correct. The person's opinion is not relevant in that matter. There is a truth—milk is white—and the same is true for moral absolutes. This reminds me of a conversation that I had once with a colleague. He expressed to me his belief that there are no absolutes—nothing that can be categorically defined as good or evil. I asked him if what he had said was an absolute statement, and he was stymied, not sure how to answer my question.

If there are moral absolutes, and, of course, there are, then we can have moral expectations of others. If there are no absolutes, then we can just go on and do our own thing, as long as we don't get caught! There are naturally long-term consequences that will eventually manifest themselves, either in our health or in our relationships. The time factor is always what causes people to believe that there will be no consequences. If nothing happens right at that moment, then some people assume they have "gotten away with" something. When they don't see any immediate consequences, they mistakenly believe that there will not be any at all.

If your truth is your truth and my truth is my truth, and those two standards of truth are diametrically opposed to one another, then in actuality there is no real standard of truth! If you decide what is right for you, and I decide what is right for me, there is no common standard upon which we can agree. This presents a problem if civility is to be expressed. For example, if we are sitting in a restaurant and your children are throwing food and carrying on as if no one else is present in the restaurant, this creates a problem for my family. This behavior may be permissible in your home, but it is disturbing and disruptive for my family in the confines of a restaurant.

Whether or not we have to appeal to the manager will depend on whether or not we can work it out between us with our collective worldviews and consensus on acceptable behavior in public places. That agreement depends on the moral foundation from which we are working. I cannot appeal to you if your set of standards differs from mine, or from the majority of law-abiding citizens. To illustrate this further, let me share a disturbing experience that I once had.

I was driving behind a pickup truck that had a young boy, perhaps eight years old, sitting in the back. He saw me and kept making signs with his fingers, especially "mister tall man!" I was upset and shocked because he kept doing it and especially because he was so young. His father pulled into a gas station, so I followed them. I got out of the car, wearing my priest's collar, and explained to the father what had been going on. The man was not embarrassed or apologetic, but simply went to the rear of the truck and told his son, "That wasn't cool!"

The father wasn't disturbed at all. He didn't ask the boy to apologize. He didn't take a moment to instruct the boy. He was not shocked and did not ask, "Where did you learn to do that? We don't do that in our family!" He didn't say, "Get out of the back of truck and ride in the front with me. We have to talk!" How do you appeal to someone who has a value system that is apparently self-protecting and who does not really care how their behavior, or their children's, affects you?

As I was observing my children playing a card game one time, I discovered that unless the rules are clearly stated, there will probably be conflict. That same principle must be applied to society, when we are talking about universals. The rules must be understood and adhered to by all in order for civility to exist. International law and the Law of War are based upon this premise and universal principles. Once the rules are made clear, anyone is free to confront other participants when they are violating the said rules. Not only are we free to do so but we also then have a moral responsibility to confront the violators of such rules.

Virtue must be encouraged in order for others to take on their moral responsibility. This encouragement must be brought on by the moral "pressure" of the community. We cannot fall back into moral relativism because then we are denying that moral truth is absolute. We have established in this chapter that a price, a moral price, must be paid by men of virtue if the moral tide in our society is going to change. Trends and fads do not lead to lasting change. What we are trying to promote is the internal growth of the moral being. This process is *impossible* unless a moral force confronts it collectively.

QUESTIONS FOR REFLECTION

1. Why has the concept of sacrifice lost value with the American public?

2. Why has American culture been deceived into believing that sacrifice is not necessary to foster moral change (an example of sacrifice being the Montgomery citizens' bus boycott in 1955 that helped desegregate the bus system in that Alabama city)?

3. Is a public sacrifice a waste or is the price that heroic men and women pay to cultivate and further public virtue worthwhile?

CHAPTER 8

WHY SOLDIERS AND POLICE PERSONNEL HAVE THE RIGHT STUFF

We have been talking about building the internal moral core of the individual, which will account for the necessary moral fiber needed to change society. Moral formation is like internal weight lifting; it must repeatedly be worked on, without missing many days, in order for it to be noticeable and successful.

In the military and in paramilitary organizations, the physical and mental training is actually an aid to moral training. In the organization I belonged to at Fort Bragg, NC, it was known as "total fitness." One was expected to be physically fit, professionally competent, and morally sound. These proficiencies are progressive, as men and women learn the visible and invisible processes, and also learn how to make the transitions through them as seamless as possible. The reason why I believe that soldiers and police personnel have the "right stuff" is due to this stated process. Let me explain further.

The kind of bravado that soldiers are trained to exhibit during combat and combat training is an indication that they are more developed in several spheres of personal growth than the average person. They are physically fit and they work diligently on being professionally competent. Because of these preparations, they are ready to push the envelope to the third sphere of moral competence, which requires serious training.

A challenge like this is nothing new to men and women who are often called upon to do the extraordinary. Men and women who practice scenario training that enables them to visualize the invisible (what they will do when confronted with unexpected and serious challenges in their work) can sometimes do what seems to be impossible to those who have not been so trained. The non-tangibles that make up virtue-building require a greater sense of community, where each individual is pursuing a standard of excellence that everyone understands and supports. It is not just those in authority who maintain the standard, it is everyone in the community who must function collectively for the process to be effective.

What is the right stuff to which I refer in this chapter's title? I will deal with this topic more comprehensively in the next chapter, but, for now, let me at least raise a question. In a land where there are few rigorous or challenging standards and it's easy to get a passing grade in almost anything with minimal effort, how does anyone know if he or she has the right stuff? When there are tryouts for the NFL draft, the scouts and coaches look for all kinds of things. They have standards that none of us who are the uninitiated would even think to look for. Then, those who are drafted have to go through training camp, where they can be observed in real life and real game situations. Some make the cut and others don't make it.

Any outfit, team, or institution worth belonging to must maintain a high standard. If that standard is compromised, the value of belonging is diminished. Why is it that high standards can be maintained in some spheres and ignored in others? It all comes down to what we as a people truly value in society. It seems that we value sports more than we value the institution of marriage, for example. The standards of performance on the football field outweigh the performance in the home by a wide margin. Those standards also surpass those for education, as evidenced by some of our communities having trouble obtaining textbooks for their students while spending billions on sports stadia. If we look past the standards and just look at the time invested in sports that could be redirected to relationships or education, one can see what our culture values.

We have identified a title for those who have not strengthened their will through moral exercise. They are referred to as weak-willed, where moral development is concerned. Are people morally responsible when they use the excuse that their lack of moral action is due to their wills being weak? Weakness in any category is due to a lack of exercise in the simplest of terms. The same is true in the arena of moral development. When people state that they are weak-willed, they are simply saying they have not exercised their will power.

Those with the right stuff do not use this as an excuse. Habit and self-mastery are necessary ingredients for those who are going to develop a strong will. People who say they are weak-willed are also implying that their will is not free! They are saying because they are not free, they cannot do as they desire. Free will by its very definition means the power to choose.

How free is free? If people believe they are predisposed to making poor moral choices due to adverse life experiences and therefore are not free to make moral decisions, does that make their will any less free than others? Absolutely not! Life's circumstances do play a part in anyone's ability to make good decisions, but those circumstances do not hinder us from making well-informed moral decisions if that is the goal we desire.

No one is born with the right stuff in its fullness. The right stuff can be compared to a baby's teeth coming in for the first time. It is a painful process, but once they are all in, the baby's potential is fully realized once the second or permanent set of teeth are in. Having the right stuff does not always mean that one will use the right stuff when it is necessary. The required character for the fireman to run into a burning building has more to do with the virtue of fortitude than it does with upper body strength. Upper body strength helps, but it is not enough! This illustration upholds the whole premise of this book: An external image of courage is not all that is required for someone to be virtuous. The inner being of a hero must be prepared for the process of moral development to be complete.

I'm sure you have heard the phrase "he has heart." This statement identifies the source of a hero's strength that goes beyond his physical prowess. The outer shell of a person can be deceiving because the appearance of a person does not necessarily reveal the true heart of a person. The consistency between image and inner substance has become a critical issue in the present American culture. The emphasis has been too much on the outward image, rather than on the essence and development of the whole person. We must re-evaluate what constitutes the right stuff and expand it beyond courage to include virtue (moral courage).

If the visible conceals a moral inner deficiency, the public can perceive virtue or integrity when none is present. When a perceived hero has to try to live up to an image, that person may not truly face up to the reality of who they are that is less than or inconsistent with that public image. No one is perfect, nor is anyone truly all that others believe him or her to be, so I am not discussing perfection here. If the person is covering up a character deficiency, however, then a re-evaluation of that person's integrity must take place by both that person and society at large.

There are two extremes in some people's understanding of human nature. One side has too high a regard for it, and the other side doesn't expect any excellence to proceed from it at all. People use that as an excuse for not attaining a high level of moral development (their thinking is "we cannot expect much from anyone") or they are pompous in thinking that they have arrived (their thinking is "we are Americans, so we are superior"). Where is the balance in this perception? Is human nature capable of attaining moral turpitude? (Moral turpitude is a legal concept in the United States and some other countries that refers to conduct that is considered contrary to community standards of justice, honesty, or good morals. This term appears in U.S. immigration law beginning in the 19th century.) Is human nature unaided by supernatural intervention capable of attaining heights of moral excellence?

These and others are the questions that we must ask ourselves, both as a culture and as individuals, if we are going to be morally responsible to make progress in this important arena. It is my contention that the right stuff is latent in the innermost recesses of the human soul, especially for those who face danger on behalf of others as a profession. The question then is: How does one cultivate it so that it can emerge when it is needed? Is humankind really predisposed for greatness or shall we all settle for mediocrity or worse in the realm of moral development?

American culture has compromised its moral standard and has not produced a moral leader of significance or person of greatness for decades because of the thinking "this is the best we can do." A truly good person is difficult to locate. I personally have met just one in my more than sixty years on this earth. When characterizing someone as good, I do not mean he or she is perfect, or a person who has never struggled with the right response to a moral dilemma. I define a good person as one who in his or her core understands what motivates them, knows their limitations, and is willing to honestly face the reality of who they are—and who they are not.

As I mentioned earlier, the slogan of the U.S. Marine Corps is "a few good men," not "a few brave men." The culture has seen brave men (and women), but it has seen few really good men. This statement is not meant to insult anyone, but to simply state the facts as I see them. The sentiment of the great French statesman Alexis de Tocqueville in the early nineteenth century was that America's greatness was found in America's goodness. What has changed in America's cultural values to cause this to be diminished and perhaps lost? Goodness is sometimes perceived as weakness; instead it should be seen as the real source of strength for both an individual and a society. It is the right stuff for which our culture longs, and to which we turn our attention in the next chapter.

QUESTIONS FOR REFLECTION

1. Is there a difference between sacrifice and discipline?

2. Does the total fitness matrix serve to aid your understanding of moral growth? Are there any similarities that I did not mention that you can see?

3. Do reasonable individuals have free will and are they therefore responsible for their actions?

CHAPTER 9

BY THE WAY, WHAT IS

THE RIGHT STUFF?

As I write this chapter, there is a story in the news of a TV photographer and his crew who were on their way to cover a story, when they encountered a burning car. When they stopped to help, they discovered the driver was a young woman. They rescued her and then found out that she was seven months pregnant. Why would they do that—stopping on their way to another assignment to risk their lives to save another? How do you think they felt when they discovered she was pregnant? That made the event even more meaningful, but it did not enter into their initial decision to stop.

That is the kind of behavior we expect of our fellow human beings. That story encapsulates so much of what we have already discussed and defined. As we proceed in this chapter, let's start by asking some more questions: "What is real, authentic, substantive, and absolute in human nature?" In other words, what is real and not manufactured or part of a public relations or image-building exercise? Reality is something that most people want to experience in one another. They are not interested in manufactured images, but rather the real picture. The philosopher might also ask the question, "What is real?" In this chapter, we want to examine what is real or should be real in those who are pursuing the right stuff professionally and physically. I am referring to what is real as the "right stuff."

I have already spent some time on the concepts of image and substance, so I will not belabor those any further. Suffice it to say that there is a problem with perception in modern society. We often see those who are on the stage or screen, or those who talk about doing right, as people with the right stuff. Sometimes we believe the person who wears a uniform automatically has the right stuff. The person with the right stuff (and not just fluff) is the person who has done the internal work to produce right actions in contrast to the person who just talks or appears to do right things. Talk is cheap and meaningless in the realm of integrity. The adage that says, "all that glitters is not gold" holds some credence in understanding what we are discussing.

One other revealing question to be asked at this point is, "What is the wrong stuff?" Perhaps by knowing what the wrong stuff is will help us more readily identify the right stuff. As an exercise to help us identity the right and wrong stuff, let's look at some villains and heroes from history to see if we can identify and reach a consensus on the necessary characteristics of those having the right stuff and those having the wrong stuff. I will include a name and you decide whether or not they had the right stuff:

1. Winston Churchill
2. Julius Caesar
3. Joan of Arc
4. Adolph Hitler
5. Abraham Lincoln
6. Joseph Stalin
7. Jesus of Nazareth
8. Socrates
9. Martin Luther King Jr.
10. Lee Harvey Oswald

That was pretty easy, wasn't it? Why was it so easy? Because, looking back, we can judge not what those people said, but what they did. And those we deem as having the right stuff did the right moral things more often than not (except for Jesus, who did them all the time!). By identifying the right stuff in others, that concept becomes tangible and clear. When you look back at the list above, what qualities were present in the list of heroes that represent the right stuff?

1. Loyalty
2. Truth-telling
3. Patriotism
4. Integrity
5. Lying
6. Stealing
7. Murdering
8. Humility
9. Lust
10. Love

The traits that are admirable and categorized as the "right stuff" in that list are easy to pick out if you have any kind of re-al-life experience. There are no gray areas where loyalty, truth-telling, patriotism, integrity, humility, and love are concerned. Do you agree with me? Or are there still gray areas that confuse the issue of moral excellence and development? Why doesn't our culture reward cowards? Why do we admire brave people? The reason is because we have discerned the moral deficiency in the one and the virtue or goodness in the other.

As stated in the last chapter and depicted by the title "Soldiers and Police Personnel Have the Right Stuff," I would like to modify that statement by saying that police and military personnel have the essential ingredients but not the complete rep-ertoire for the right stuff. In preparing a soup or a stew, the in-gredients are present but the stew is not quite complete. It needs perhaps three or four hours to simmer or marinate in order to qualify as a soup or a stew. Potential is not the same as fruition, and fruition requires time.

In the arena of martial arts, a white belt (a beginner) and a black belt (a teacher of sorts) are both considered martial artists. A new officer and a seasoned officer are both considered police officers. The Army used to frame what I am talking about with the phrase, "be all that you can be." In other words, they were saying that Army leaders needed to simmer or stew over time, just like that pot of soup, in order to reach their full potential.

The right stuff is what counters the wrong stuff. Evildoers (not purely evil people) have all the wrong stuff working for and in them. Good people (not in essence, but in action) have the right stuff at their disposal. Can we function in the categories of right and wrong at the same time? Is it wrong to steal? Is it right to share? The road that distinguishes one from goodness to greatness is covered with choices that require prudence instead of passion.

Most virtue warriors have jobs that expose them frequently to the public, and they are constantly under scrutiny while encountering a myriad of challenges and societal problems that few have faced. What I am about to say may sound simplistic and perhaps outdated, but the private life and the public life of the virtue warrior flow together and spill over one into the other. If there is duplicity in private life, then it will eventually show up in their public life. If a policeman, for example, is abusing his wife, he will not hesitate to abuse the public when certain situations trigger that response. Therefore, a virtuous private life is part of the right stuff.

Stephen Mansfield illustrates this in his book about the life of Winston Churchill, entitled *Never Give In*. Mansfield explains how mores have changed considerably in just one generation. Under the rubric of marriage, he states:

> We no longer live when public men are measured by the quality of their marriages. 'Men of affairs' today

are often just that and the greater the distance they can place between themselves and their crumbling home lives, the better. For some unclear reason, the inability of a man to loyally fulfill his vows to his wife is no longer taken as indication of the character with which he will serve the public (Mansfield, p. 110).

The hidden or private life is often more important than the public life because it reveals the true integrity of a person. When a person is essentially the same person in the dark (private or hidden life) as he or she is in the light (public life), it can safely be said that the person possesses integrity and has the right stuff. An integer in math is a whole number, and wholeness is the best definition for integrity, because when people are integrated (their private and public lives are whole because they live their values when everyone and no one is watching), there is no deficiency in their character. When people segregate their conduct, living one way in public and another way in private, they are living a double life that reveals duplicity and that is the breeding ground for the wrong stuff.

This condition of duplicity is definitely not the right stuff. If people are consistently true to who they are and not to just what they are *expected* to do, they will not be in danger of living a double life. In his book *The Many Faces of Virtue*, Donald Demarco has this to say about integrity, "Multiplicity is fragmentation, fractionalization, dispersion, and dividedness. It is captured in the colloquial expression 'going to pieces.'" (DeMarco, p. 200).

This brings us back to the statement by Socrates, which is "know thyself." Only truly honest individuals can know who they really are. A self-deprecating person may not be accurate in their assessment either, for that may be part of their duplicity. They portray themselves as humble, but could have a raging pride burning inside that only those closest to them can see. In order for people to be objective as to who they truly are, they will need the help of others who are truly committed to their success in the realm of moral development. Those mentors or coaches can help individuals identify their moral blind spots, and assist them in being honest when their judgment may be clouded due to internal conflict or external pressures to perform according to a certain standard.

Those who really possess the right stuff can impart those qualities to others by instruction and through mentoring and teaching opportunities. People pick up the habits of those around them, whether good or bad ones. The old adage that declares your friends reveal your character is a true statement. We are drawn to others who have characteristics that we ourselves value. Those with the right stuff usually hang around others who have the right stuff. Those with the wrong stuff usually find others who are losers as well. Winners seek out other winners, losers seek out other losers.

It is perhaps time to re-evaluate the company you keep if you really want to grow in virtue. When competing in sports, it is usually better to compete against someone better than yourself. By doing so, your skill will more than likely improve. It is the same with character development. The company you keep should be "better" so you can grow. The tendency may be to associate with people who are your moral inferiors so that no challenge is presented to your own level of development.

When searching out a mentor, you should look at the qualities that you desire to acquire before making a commitment to share your life with an individual. Habits take a lifetime to master in the realm of moral development, so one must be sure that the mentor possesses these qualities and is not just talking about them. It is all too easy to have the impression that if one *knows* about virtue, then that person must *possess* it. This can lead to deception and disappointment.

Self-deception occurs when people believe something to be true about themselves when it is not true. This is a serious pitfall when it has to do with one's own moral development. Blind spots are difficult to see without the aid of others, especially when one believes he or she possesses the right stuff.

For example, the physical qualifications (and some psychological tests) don't always take into account the character qualities that are essential for certain professional positions. The medical doctor may be proficient as a surgeon, but may also have a drinking problem, and this disqualifies him when it comes to trustworthiness. Good grades acquired in medical school do not guarantee that the doctor is making the grades years later. Would you want to be operated on by a doctor who may have been binge drinking the night before? They may even deceive themselves that they can "handle it," only to be proved wrong in a series of operations. This is why one's personal and professional life enters into the mix for the right stuff.

Firemen and police personnel must not only maintain their proficiency, but they must also continually prove that they have the right stuff. The champion stock car racer who is 50 years old must prove that he or she still has the instincts to drive in such a competitive field. If they do not, then everyone will be in danger due to possible negligence and skill erosion. When this happens, professionals can cross the line of moral excellence into moral confusion and baseness. The right stuff becomes the wrong stuff when the right stuff is no longer exercised or when it stops developing.

What's more, who cares for the caregiver? Does the doctor ever need a doctor? How about mental health professionals? Are there ever times when they need a respite, a chance to reflect on where they are personally and professionally, identifying moral areas where they need to learn and grow? The right stuff continually needs to be cultivated in all virtue warriors, just like a garden. If a garden isn't "cared for," it will suffer from over exposure to the elements, the soil will be depleted, the weeds will choke out the good plants, or the future crops will be meager or even fail. The same is true for leaders in all professions. Even knowing when to leave a job or a professional position will help people recognize their ethical limitations and also help them stay proficient in their cluster of critical job skills.

The right stuff can go bad without practice; don't assume that you will always have it. Police officers must keep going to the pistol range to maintain and perhaps even improve their accuracy and proficiency. Soldiers and police officers must do the same where goodness and moral issues are concerned. If they don't, they will begin to misuse the great gift God gave human beings, and that is the gift of rational thinking. Let's turn to that topic in our next chapter.

QUESTIONS FOR REFLECTION

1. Who in your life has the stuff? How is it recognizable?

2. Why is it important to be able to discriminate (perceive or constitute the difference) between good and evil or good and bad?

3. What heroes and what villains come to your mind who are not on the lists that I presented above? Note: they do not have to be historical figures, but may be people you work with, live with or know right now.

CHAPTER 10

MAN:

THE RATIONAL ANIMAL

Reason, or basically how we think, must help us harness our vices in order to overcome the passionate side. In other words, our thinking must partner with our emotions, or else the emotions will tend to rule our lives. Passion and emotion are not evil, but if your life is dominated by them, you are not totally free to be rational. Thinking and feeling should both be present, with thinking dominating the two in most cases. In professional work, where thinking on one's feet is important, passion (emotions) or fear cannot cloud the need to think clearly, especially in police work.

Humans possess the ability to reason, whereas lower animals live mostly by instinct. Humans reflect on what is reasonable more often than they instinctively rely on their physical senses to know right from wrong. Natural Law recognizes that humans are hard-wired to "know" right from wrong, but because of negligence, most people are not ready to follow their moral inclinations. Has something gone awry in the mechanism? Is it not working as designed? No, it is working, but it must be cultivated, and reason will enhance the process. Reason is a powerful tool used successfully by rational people who have learned to distinguish between passion and principle.

It is essential that we learn to rationally process our emotional responses. Before you compromise or violate one of your life values, demand that you give yourself good reasons as to why this decision is correct. If you cannot, then reconsider the path you are contemplating. Don't fall back on the adage "the heart has its reasons" because sometimes that sentiment is not always rational! Consider these words from a moral guide for children, one from which I was instructed as a child: "The human virtues are stable dispositions of the intellect and the will that govern our acts, order our passions, and guide our conduct" (Baltimore Catechism). If that is not true, then our lives are often chaotic, subject to the whims of our emotional inclinations.

We must all discipline our passions so that our being is not in disorder and disarray. It is rational to give, while it is irrational to steal. It is logical and rational to tell the truth, while it is highly irrational to tell a lie and deceive. It is rational to save a life, while it is highly irrational to destroy a life for no reason. Ethics is sometimes defined as *recta ratio agibilium*, the science of human action in which reason enables us to determine the correct ethical course that must be taken. What is needed in moral development is correct and not erroneous reasoning, for the latter will have severe repercussions and consequences. The truth that there are consequences to all our actions seems to be lost in modern society; however, it is reasonable to believe that such a reality, also known as the law of reaping and sowing, exists.

The lower animals are not able to rationalize along these lines. Perhaps they can discern when something is too hot to eat or drink, but rationalizing is limited from there. By contrast, the moral animal (human beings) has many other capacities that come into play when making moral decisions, such as considering the consequences to others that may come from our choices. Rationale, or the ability to make good judgments, is also a component not considered when discussing the lower animals or the underdeveloped moral human. Reason, which is considered by some to be the highest faculty of the soul, is rightly ordered when good moral decisions are made. Reason must direct and re-direct the passions if the moral human is to live above mere instinct.

I am not denying the existence or usefulness of what we often refer to as intuition. Intuition is a sense that resides in someone of what should or should not be done, and rational reasons cannot always be articulated. Yet intuition is not infallible and is actually more effective when it has been developed and shaped. This is inconsistent with the image of intuition that many hold that intuition is purely subjective and a random, unexplained feeling. Let me give an example.

Let's say a fireman is in a burning house and suddenly senses it's time to get out. Right after he or she does, the floor collapses. That is intuition, but in all probability, that intuition was honed through experience and paying attention to the little things: the sounds, the heat, the direction the flames were moving, and any number of other conditions. While that feeling to vacate was intuition, it did not exist or develop in a vacuum. It was based on the development of the fire fighter's rational side, which can even function when the fireman is preoccupied.

As a moral animal, I am more than mere instinct. Instinct is good to have as well as intuition, but those cannot replace reason as dominant in moral decision-making. Intellect must inform the seat of passions, which is sometimes called the heart. If the heart dictates and suppresses the intellect, the outcome of decisions will not be considered rational. As a moral animal, I can dominate my lower cravings and harness my passions by utilizing the power of my will. In that way, I am not enslaved by the power of my passions and can make a superior moral judgment. I can still be passionate, but I am not mastered by my passions!

The natural lower instincts that are often referred to as the tendency to fight or flight are present in the moral animal but moral training can teach the moral animal to live above mere instinct. General George Patton once said, "Do not take counsel of your fears." The same concept is present during the accomplishment of heroic acts. Fear says, "Don't go into a burning building to save lives," but training says, "Put the fear in check and do the noble and courageous thing." To be dominated by fear is to be held captive by one's emotional life rather than to one's rational inclinations.

Fear many times is a lie captivating the one who fears with concerns that are not likely to happen. Risk-taking is a part of life. To challenge your fears reduces the concern down to its most reasonable outcome if things don't work out. For example, if I do what is in my heart, I may fail but I may learn something to avoid the same mistake in the future. If I take the risk, I may lose some money or I may be set back in my pursuit of a career goal. Can I live with that? If I can, then I have an incentive and reason to overcome the fear, and move forward.

Yet, if pursuing my risk, I may lose my life, then that is another level of risk that I must consider. If that result is not worth the risk, then I should back off the challenge. If it is in the context of saving a loved one (I give my life to protect theirs), then that risk may be assessed as reasonable and important. If the risk is to accomplish some worthless achievement, then that risk is not rational. The key is to visualize the appropriate result with the risk and then assess the worth of the possible loss versus the possible gain.

If there is no risk-taking, there cannot be any victory or excitement that comes with living life on the edge! I am not advocating foolishness, but our lives must count for something. Either we will be people of rational abandon or people who live in the shadow of fear. Consider this question: "Head or heart? Who should be king or queen in the life of a rational but passionate individual?" I do not negate the reality or worth of feelings and intuition. In my opinion, however, they are too nebulous and unpredictable a foundation upon which to build a moral and ethical life.

To be reasonable means to give good reasons for a decision that is being made, reasons that make sense and can hold up to the scrutiny of logic. Passions can defy reason and often cause disastrous outcomes, especially when "love" and "lust" are involved. We often talk about chemistry where relationships and teams are concerned. When I was away from home in the military, I saw a man who was married but who had fallen in love and was involved with another woman. They claimed the chemistry was there, but the chemistry was overriding his rational commitment he should have maintained to his spouse back home.

A team can have chemistry, but if someone heads the team for an exercise that risks lives because that person is not qualified, then the chemistry of the team caused them to make the wrong decision. Chemistry is not the same thing as rationality; the distinction must be made in good decision-making exercises. Chemistry is "real" but limited in its ability to speak logically to a rational individual.

Cognitive powers can evaluate feelings and sensations and see if they pass the common sense (which is not too common) test. For example, if a police team is ready to break down the door, common sense says they want the strongest men, not the smaller persons in the front. That decision passes the common sense test. Emotional people tend to cave in psychologically when not directed by a more stable moral compass than their feelings when making life-impacting decisions. A well-thought-out truth is superior to a feeling with no basis in rational thought.

Humans are rational animals and should predominately function in the realm of reason if they are going to be ethically victorious in their decision making. The capacity to reason is exclusive to the human species and should be utilized so that humans can provide sound direction and care for the world. Compassion and feelings are also necessary and must be considered (these comprise empathy), but detachment from these feelings is necessary to have a clear mind to make rational decisions.

How often have parents heard children say, "I don't feel like it"? In parental training, children are taught to live above their feelings in order to be successful in life and in their careers. Without this discipline, children would be unmotivated and unable to face the harsh realities of life. Living above their feelings is not just a stoic way of coping with life's challenges, it is the way of survival if one is to succeed through mental discipline.

People who possess all good will and no common sense will not produce lasting results. Don't think for one minute that Mother Saint Teresa of Calcutta was just a compassionate person with no head on her shoulders, for the evidence indicates otherwise. She was a thoughtful person whose heart was moved by human misery and whose head was directed with sound organizational skills (to plan) and self-discipline, which were evidenced by her strict adherence to the rules of her Order.

Feeling is not enough; action must implement a plan that will relieve the pain being observed that others are suffering. Social action is just that—*action*—and not simply social rhetoric. Social justice comes with a plan that will provide longevity to the justice that is being implemented. G.K. Chesterson (1874-1936) made an interesting comment about the faculty of reason: "I am unable to imagine any human being accepting any authority that he has not originally reached by reason." Chesterton was a great writer, thinker, and religionist who applied this principle to all facets of his life.

While serving on an honors board for those who had violated the honor code in the U.S. Army, I was asked to judge the circumstances with this dictum: "What would a *reasonable* person think about this situation?" They did not ask me to judge what a feeling, sensitive person would have done in that potential violation of the honor code. They wanted to know what a reasonable person would do. I found that interesting.

As in other realms where judgment is necessary, the more one does something, the better one becomes at it. The rational man or woman, by exercising their judgment, will perfect it by regular and appropriate use. When a team of reasonable people is pursuing the same ends, moral consensus will more than likely be the outcome.

Reasonable people have established reliable guidelines for making consistent moral decisions. People who exclusively or primarily function in the emotional realm do not always use logic to come to their conclusions; therefore, many times their decisions have no consistency. Rational people make their emotions subservient to the collective factors that make up the human personality. When reason dictates the moral decisions that one makes, those decisions contribute to the overall civility of humanity.

"That was a reasonable choice" is more desirable than hearing "that was an emotional choice," in most cases. When a person can be reasoned with (because they still possess cognition to make a moral decision), a reasonable person has more of a chance of convincing the irascible (having or showing a tendency to be easily angered) person of their deficiency. Knowing what your passion is in life is not the same thing as being ruled by the passions. The former has to do with purpose whereas the latter has to do with sentiment ruling the whole being. The end result undoubtedly remains that the passions must be ruled by reason or one ceases to be reasonable.

QUESTIONS FOR REFLECTION

1. How would you define a reasonable person?
2. Why is it important to rely more on logic than feeling in a professional setting?
3. Does it serve the public interest for you to be stoic in an emergency situation as a public servant?

CHAPTER 11

THE "MANLINESS" REQUIRED TO ACQUIRE VIRTUE

A famous saying in an ancient document encourages its adherents to "act like men," even though those adherents were both male and female. In being faithful to the cultural interpretation of that document, one must not politicize the statement by putting a twenty-first century nuance on its meaning. The same paradigm shift is necessary if one is going to understand the content of this chapter. Manliness is not about gender; it's about what we used to call fiber—the moral fiber that involved courage and the willingness to do what is right.

There is a scene in *The Godfather*, in which Don Corleone slaps his godson across the face for not having the fortitude to face his life crisis. That is an example of manliness. The controversial decision of General George Patton to slap a frightened soldier was the General's misguided attempt to challenge the young soldier's manhood. Teaching someone to act courageously in the face of crisis must be something that is ingrained in that person for many years before it is tested, regardless of whether they are male or female.

Please understand from the start that I am not advocating violence. Instead, I am encouraging strength of character so that those who are called to influence can do a better job. Nurturing has its place in moral development, but so does having a stiff upper lip. If the fortitude necessary to develop virtue is not consistently present in the life of an emergent leader or public servant, virtue will not mature or come to fruition. Inner strength will harness the inner qualities necessary for a man or woman to become a person of virtue. Just like anything else worth attaining, one has to work at it! Character formation, not simply cognitive information, is the task at hand.

Virtue, as stated earlier, has its roots in the word *virile*. Strength is what is required if character is going to be formed and not just informed. There is a perception in American culture, however, that the moral capacity is not present to achieve such a goal. Consequently, it is almost never seriously pursued. If a person rode a bicycle for 20 miles every day for a month, it would make sense that this person would eventually develop strong leg muscles. On the other hand, if someone told the absolute truth for thirty days, we would doubt whether a moral habit of truth-telling had really been formed. For some reason, some in our modern culture refuse to accept this notion of moral capacity or development. The goal here is not just to stop lying, but instead to speak the truth consistently for at least thirty days. Moral development can be likened to internal exercise. Virtue will emerge if one consistently works the program.

Why has modern culture refused to try? Here are some suggestions as to the answer:

1. Fear of failure
2. It's not cool to be a "goody-two-shoes."
3. Deep in one's heart, one does not want to be virtuous.
4. The hedonistic tendencies of the culture
5. Pure laziness

Does a person like Mother Saint Teresa of Calcutta have a different DNA that gives her a proclivity toward goodness, or does every reasonable person begin at the same place that she began? We have lied to ourselves (although we have secretly admired virtuous people) that we are not capable and therefore have sold ourselves short of our potential. It is said that God doesn't make junk, so how could those He created not have within them the capacity to be and do good?

We are all capable of becoming better, but if virtue cultivation is neglected, we will become worse for lack of use. What does a morally developed people look like?

1. They are consistent in their actions, revealing their maturity.

2. They have internalized moral habits, so therefore character has been etched on their souls.

3. They do not desire to be evil-doers, but instead grieve over injustice.

4. They are always seeking to grow morally and ethically.

A person who is improving physically normally attends a gym, a person who is improving intellectually usually attends a university, but where does a person go to improve morally? We must surround ourselves with others who have the same goals (perhaps for different reasons, for people attend the gym to achieve all kinds of personal objectives) where morality is concerned. I used to tell my children "Church, library, gym." They would never be the person God intended them to be if they became one-dimensional in any of those three areas. Moral development is not often deliberate and most people think they received all they needed at home while growing up, for good or bad.

If people were raised in a Christian home, they can wrongly assume they got all the moral development they needed by living in that home. That is incorrect. They had a good foundation, but they need to continue their development. Also, grown children often react and rebel against what their parents taught them. If the parental teaching was bad or immoral, then those children are acting correctly to rebel, but if they are in rebellion to their proper upbringing, then their moral training is going in the wrong direction.

According to Aristotle, the young are not always ready to undergo the painstaking effort required to attain virtue, and, quite frankly, many of them are simply not interested. Therefore, one is not a finished product by the age of 25! Although it is harder to begin to develop morally at that age, the individual is usually mentally more prepared for change in their twenties. Don't get me wrong; moral development must take place throughout the formative years, but the necessary cooperation does not usually take place until the person is 25 years of age, and in some cases in American society, even later! Young people are usually driven by the fact that "they are never going to die" and have a greater investment in their material things and "toys" than in their moral legacy.

The fact that life is not a dress rehearsal, but the final act, should give one pause. I have used an exercise on the university level that is, to some, a bit morbid (although police personnel and soldiers think about it more often than most). This exercise asks, "What do you want engraved on your tombstone?" At first, it is disconcerting to some, but then they begin to think about the answer. The answers they share are many times inconsistent with the lifestyles that many in the class are pursuing. I know this because of my relationship as confidante with many of them. This inconsistency must be corrected. Whatever they want others to see on their tombstone must be lived out, not later but now, for they are not guaranteed that they will live to see "later."

People can only start the repair if they know where they really are, and that brings us back to the maxim proposed by Socrates: "Know thyself—an unexamined life is not worth living."

That is an exhortation to truly know yourself and not just know about your basic physical characteristics. It means to comprehend your internal being so that your shortcomings can be addressed and confronted with the truth about who you truly are, not who you want to be or who others think you are. In the next chapter, we will spend more time with the concept of moral work, which one man likened to swimming in peanut butter, which requires constant effort. Manliness, strength of character, and constant effort will allow the student of virtue to acquire maturity.

This truth is why I appreciate the sacrament of confession. It causes me to realistically and regularly self-evaluate, so as not to project myself to be more than I am. It keeps me grounded and gives me direction for where I need to improve. It also puts me in touch with God's grace, which I realize I need to continue the process.

Joan of Arc (1412-1431) was a virtuous and courageous young woman. If you are not familiar with the true story about Saint Joan of Arc, you owe it to yourself to search the annals of history and read it. It is a story of profound courage and faith that changed the course of a nation. Her feats had nothing to do with gender, but, instead, with extraordinary character. Her strength was inner and therefore became manifest in more tangible ways. Even though many centuries have passed since she lived, the court records of her trial have been preserved.

Joan summed up the quality that I have been talking about when she addressed the French captains by saying: "Fear not, however many they be! Neither weigh difficulties. God guides our work. Were I not certain that God guides this work, I would rather keep sheep than expose myself to such perils" (*The Gnostic Muse* site).

Mark Twain (Samuel L. Clemens) has done a comprehensive work on Joan's life that required twelve years to research and two years to write. It was his assessment that no other work of his required that kind of attention. Sir Winston Churchill has also written favorably about Joan's actions (even though his country of Britain was on the losing side of her war-like spirit) in his outstanding *History of the English Speaking Peoples*. Acting like men does not mean to act mannish if you are feminine. It does encompass, however, a courageous spirit that has nothing to do with gender.

Becoming virtuous comes with a high price to those who are morally underdeveloped because of their stunted growth. Instead of being responsible moral agents, however, it is in vogue to blame everyone else for moral failures. These excuses cripple peoples free will and their ability to choose the path they want for themselves. The old adage that "the devil made me do it" is still used widely today by morally irresponsible people, even if they don't recognize the devil's existence!

We will not discuss evil and its source at this point in time. It is important to remember, however, that no matter how thin you slice baloney, it always has two sides! The weak-willed, rather than exercising their underdeveloped wills, cave in to their lower appetites. The lower appetites are instinctive but should not be the dominant force in the life of an individual if they wish to develop morally.

These lower appetites are necessary, but the mastery of them is even more necessary due to the enslavement they can produce if left unchecked. Life is about moderation and should be lived within the confines of extremes. To control one's anger, to hold one's tongue, and to master one's passions are all challenges civilized people face in order to maintain a decent and virtuous life. If these harnesses and checks are ignored, extremes will develop and they will be difficult to break free from when one is seeking a more moderate lifestyle.

In ancient times, a charioteer had several horses connected to his chariot. He was trying to utilize the power of those horses to win a race, fight a battle, or reach a destination. He could not have those horses run wild, but he needed their power to be under control so they would respond to his direction. The same is true for our passions, which have been referred to as the seven deadly sins of pride, greed, lust, anger, gluttony, envy, and sloth. They must be under control or they will take the chariot of our lives in dangerous directions.

If those deadly sins, to which it is possible for all people to succumb, are not harnessed, it will lead to a life gone astray morally. If they are confronted, harnessed, and redirected, however, they can be transformed into the seven capital virtues of humility, liberality, chastity, mildness, temperance, happiness, and diligence. Study those two lists. Which list is more heroic, more to be admired, more desired to be incorporated into a moral life? With whom would you rather partner, someone who has given into the deadly sins or someone who has developed the cardinal virtues? The answer should be obvious.

The habits produced during youth usually stay with an individual unless a radical change occurs to alter his or her life. A change of life like that is rare, but it is not impossible, especially if one is serious about self-awareness and self-improvement. Self-improvement can often be aided by mutual improvement, which occurs when another person assists you as you attempt to grow in virtue. This help does not come in the form of criticism but in reinforcing the virtues you desire to possess.

Most of the time, the person helping already possesses these same virtues and usually values the same characteristics in others that you do. Having a companion during an exercise run usually pushes one or both of the participants, or it simply keeps them accountable in remaining committed to the exercise regimen. This illustration can carry over to the development of virtue as well, because competition is not always bad even between the best of friends. When we try to outdo one another, we may both become better because of our mutual effort. The old adage that says, "Good, better, best, never let them rest, until your good is better and your better is best" is very appropriate at this juncture in this discussion. Never settle for good if you can reach better, and never settle for better if you can attain best! This philosophy and practice will lead us into our next chapter, where you will learn how to swim in peanut butter!

QUESTIONS FOR REFLECTION

1. Are you convinced that people can develop morally? Why or why not?

2. Do you understand the concept of manliness as something that men and women of virtue must possess? Explain your answer.

3. What does it mean to be morally self-aware? Are you clear on the concept that self-awareness leads to moral development?

CHAPTER 12

LEARNING TO SWIM IN PEANUT BUTTER

Have you ever done something that was especially difficult, but after you accomplished it, you felt the better for having done it? The challenge I will propose in this chapter will be similar to that experience. Rev. Bob Mumford first mentioned the metaphor about swimming in peanut butter (which has greatly enriched my life with insight and illumination about the virtue process) many years ago when I heard him speak at a conference. It has helped me understand that constant effort is necessary to develop lasting habits. If you have ever gone on a long road march, you know that there is a rhythm that develops. You also know that the way to reach your destination is to put one foot in front of the other and then repeat the process for thousands upon thousands of steps. There is no glory connected to it, not even a rush of achievement, but what is there instead is a pace that will get you to the finish line. You can run most of it, you can even crawl some of it, but if you develop a consistent pace (a kind of cadence), the chances of finishing are improved.

Why do people have moral failures? Why do character facades only last for a season? If one is a moral actor rather than a moral champion, the oil in the machine of the actor is going to run out eventually. Why are Americans so hung up on what they do rather than on what they are? In actuality, it is easier to do something rather than to become something that is lasting and will leave a legacy. If I were to ask you, "What do you do?" it would be much easier to answer than if I asked you, "What have you become?"

Someone has said that the face you have at age of fifty is the face you have earned. Some folks cannot smile very often because they have had very little practice. Some people cannot stop smiling because it has been a way of life for them. Practice makes perfect or better yet, perfect practice makes perfect. If you have ever been at a ceremony or at a lecture, you can very quickly tell whether or not the person or persons have diligently practiced that of which they speak. If they have not, it shows in the performance. If they have, it shows in the excellence and confidence that are exhibited in their presentation. Learning to be consistent in one's behavior comes with rigorous practice. Bad habits are hard to break, but if you stop with the breaking of a bad habit and do not develop a good habit to replace it, the process is incomplete.

It is my understanding that the way they got "Mister Ed" (the talking horse) to look like he was actually talking was to put peanut butter on the roof of his mouth! The effort trying to get some peanut butter off the roof of his mouth proved to be a challenge to him, but not an impossible task. Swimming in peanut butter (building character) will offer the same challenge to those who wish to pursue it.

The path of least resistance has been the path that has been chosen by many for this very reason. It is easier to take and, for the most part, there are no major sacrifices to make. We live in a culture that wants everything yesterday, if not sooner. We want degrees accomplished in no time, houses built overnight, and relationships to flourish without adequate time to grow. So when we don't see character forming quickly, we accept the lie that it is an impossible task. If you have been lying consistently for twenty years, it will take longer than two weeks to break the old habit and substitute a new one.

Most people like a challenge. Recently, on the news, I heard a plea for 500 men to become Navy Seals. They were offering a large bonus, but then they explained that the Seal recruits get only about 4 hours of sleep a week during their intense training. Everyone wants the glory, but not many want to produce the guts. The success rate in 2006 for those desiring to be Seals was 32%. That isn't too high, but was actually improving over what it had been. It was stated that they couldn't lower the bar due to the nature of the mission.

We admire woodcarvings and exotic furniture in cathedrals that took perhaps hundreds of years to erect. The making of a soul that will live forever, however, must be given at least as much attention toward its development. The body will break down eventually and the mind will fail at times, but the component that is eternal deserves the most attention because it lives on forever. In my estimation, the body needs the gym, the mind needs the academy, and the soul needs the Church. Moral development does not take place in a vacuum. If one wants to be virtuous, one must search out virtuous people who already possess the qualities desired. The old adage that says, "bad company corrupts good morals" is true, but the opposite can be true as well. Good company can encourage and help develop good morals.

Learning is a process and learning to swim in peanut butter is a difficult one. Strain and struggle oftentimes strengthen a weakness in a person's body, and the same is true for the reconstruction of the soul. Some would protest that the texture of peanut butter forbids it from being a liquid that one can swim in; that observation is accurate to the average person who is not looking to do anything extraordinary. To the visionary who believes in greatness, however, they see it as a challenge.

As we study the "habits" (in the Aristotelian sense) of great women and men in history, one discovers that they were not ordinary people when it came to the formation of their habits. Whether it was George Washington, with his rules of civility, or the habits and practices of Mahatma Gandhi, their greatness was the result of the foundation they laid through their habits. Gandhi described seven dangers to human virtue, and they are: 1) wealth without work; 2) pleasure without conscience; 3) knowledge without character; 4) business without ethics; 5) science without humanity; 6) religion without sacrifice; and 7) politics without principles.

Those two men, along with many other moral giants, were all peanut butter swimmers! What makes a peanut butter swimmer you may ask? It is a person who will not settle for mediocrity, but instead wants to reach his or her full moral potential. In the Aristotelian sense, a word that we translate as *happiness* for Aristotle meant "to flourish and reach one's human potential." One's purpose or teleology is the ultimate end or goal of one's life when it reaches its full potential.

Destiny is not a word that most people are comfortable talking about, especially when it has to do with their own lives and purpose. If people saw, for instance, that their purpose in life was to be Olympic athletes, would this have an effect on their daily discipline and practice habits? It certainly would and if neglected, it would greatly alter their telos or ultimate goal. Are there people who feel a "call" to do what others consider impossible? Risk takers or peanut butter swimmers have heard the objections of many critics (who have probably not taken many calculated risks in their own lives), but they refuse to look back on their lives and say, "I was too afraid to live my dream" or "I wasn't willing to pay the price for my dream."

These regrets are too common in people who have settled for less in life and have given up their dreams. I have spoken to people who transfer their dreams to the next generation, which in essence is a relinquishment of their God-given responsibility.

They live through their children or grandchildren, choosing not to live for themselves. Unfulfilled dreams, or worse yet, watching others fulfill the dreams you believed were yours, can be a disconcerting experience in the life of a potential peanut butter swimmer.

But you may think, "Isn't swimming in peanut butter messy?" My answer is yes, but isn't the birth of a child "messy" also? We call the birth of a child a beautiful experience, which is repeated irrespective of the pain. (I will admit that God, in His goodness, has provided some "motivation" to keep the species reproducing!) The rearing of these same children, however, is the real challenge, yet the human race continues to replenish. Potential in children is a sign of the human capacity that is just waiting to be cultivated. Some cultivate it and others waste their God-given talents and opportunities. My challenge to you is this: Jump into the peanut butter pool and experience the warmth and pliable environment that in the long run has the potential to make you into a champion!

QUESTIONS FOR REFLECTION

1. Do you agree that moral development is a lifetime pursuit? What implications does that have for you?
2. Go back and find Aristotle's definition of happiness. Is that your definition as well? What do you believe your ultimate purpose is?
3. Is there a risk involved in moral development? What can it cost to be a virtuous person?

CHAPTER 13

WHAT WILL

THE WORLD LOOK LIKE

WITH VIRTUOUS MEN?

What does the world look like now? I remember viewing a *Honeymooners* TV show, starring Jackie Gleason, when Gleason (Ralph) informed his wife that the world was a man's world, run by men, led by men. I will never forget his wife Alice's reply, "How are they doing?" In a male-dominated world (at least the last century and preceding), what has characterized the world? A careful study of history will reveal one thing—wars! Were those wars planned and led by women or men?

I don't need a lesson in physiology. I understand that due to muscle mass, most men are physically stronger than most women. Men have dominated women not by their charm, but instead by their muscle density. Women have been given the chance to prove themselves in the last half-century in many spheres and, for the most part, they have not proven to be morally superior to men. Historically, women have been perceived as more virtuous than men, but that, unfortunately, is quickly changing.

Heroic virtues have excused valiant men and they have

received a pass on moral issues for the most part. Therefore, due to our present state, we really do not know what the world would look like with truly virtuous men. Let's dream for a moment— but before we do, let me state emphatically that I believe mankind to be defective (in theological terms, it means humankind is sin sick or possesses what is commonly called "original sin"). Total perfection is not within the reach of humankind but even though humankind is wounded, it does not mean humankind is hopeless. Humankind may be helpless at times, but humankind is never hopeless! Striving for perfection is not a futile task, but it must be modified so that disillusionment does not set in.

How does the world look now? There is violent crime perpetrated, for the most part, by men. There are sexual sins, such as rape and pedophilia, which are also mostly perpetrated by men. Greed appearing as white-collar crime, has also traditionally been performed by the male gender. Power abuse, also carried out by men due to their aggressive nature, has subjected tribes and peoples to slavery. Pleasure (the obsession that men have to sports and gambling) has deprived families of the attention of their husbands and fathers. These excesses have blurred the focus of what is really important in life, and have also contributed to the hedonistic culture that America is slowly adopting.

All is not hopeless or dark. Philanthropy is alive and well, as illustrated by the lives of Bill Gates, Oprah Winfrey, and the past giants of industry (men like Carnegie and Rockefeller), whom we have also referred to as "robber barons." These people have used the excesses of their productivity to change the world and should give us some hope, but the present moral climate of America does not look good. This can change, however, if men will put down their toys and start rebuilding civilization for the future.

What would the world look like with virtuous men? First, it would be peaceful because it would be guarded by men rather than harassed by them. It would be pure because men would guard the purity of their loved ones and penalize those who would try to violate them. Power would be tempered with compassion because money, sex, and power would not be the motivations behind progress. Finally, philanthropy would change the ills of the world due to the generous nature of humankind.

Has there ever been such a utopia? Are these goals even remotely possible? These are valid questions that need to be answered in light of the quality of life, dignity, and civility that many Americans still pursue. Questions and answers are important as we deliberate problems, but action is the need of the day. Virtuous goals motivate virtuous men.

"How can I make my world a better place?" should be their guiding question. As stated before, "evil prevails when good men do nothing." Virtuous men must act! Small actions are a good start rather than no action at all. There is the tendency in our culture to talk things to death and do nothing, or to wait until we can do something big. I have a friend who says he didn't give $10 to a need because it wasn't $100. His point was that he often withheld the good he could do because it wasn't very significant in his own estimation. That's the wrong way to think. We must all do what we can where we are for a moral community and country to emerge.

How do we change from being talking machines to performers? The world would be a better place if everyone concentrated on his or her own sphere of responsibility: "You clean your yard and I'll clean mine." This would greatly aid the landscape problem and the litter problem as well. Dealing with the pollution that emits from your vehicle is your problem until it becomes mine. The behavior of your family members resides at your address before it affects others. So virtuous men can start small and then unite their efforts and collectively do great things.

Consider organizing a crime watch team that simply informs the police and is not some makeshift para-police organization. Things should not be done for glory or notoriety, but instead for the common good. Virtuous men and women want to see virtue in action, whether it is a show of courage or an act of kindness. They refuse to stand by and watch our culture die.

Let's try and visualize virtue. Many of us have had the unfortunate experience of witnessing and experiencing the effects of vice. We have seen vice in our inner cities, schools, and in big business. Virtue, however, has reared its beautiful head (sometimes unnoticed) at different times in history but unfortunately, not long enough to have a lasting effect. Every once in a while we are given a glimpse, however, of beauty, truth, and goodness in the life of an individual. These instances assure us that it is truly possible to attain to such moral heights.

One lone individual is commendable, but if you can visualize with me an entire community committed to this kind of lifestyle, it would be a significant achievement. It is common knowledge that decent people have gotten fed up with the increase in crime. People get angry, but they don't do anything about it except complain to each other, call a talk show, or write a letter to the editor. Those actions or inactions do not remedy the problem; they only exacerbate it.

As stated earlier, we cannot change others, but we can work on ourselves. We can take care of our little part of the world, and then our enthusiasm might become contagious and spur others to action! We are not talking about creating some symbolic effort that will make others feel better. We are trying to activate all good men and women who realize they can make a difference in this moral mess if they get involved right where they are.

Politicians are not equipped to produce such change—it must come from the people and represent a revolution of *virtue!* I hope you join me in wanting to feel safe walking the streets in our inner cities once again. It is almost out of the question to visit some neighborhoods to share our nostalgia with our family members due to the fact that those areas have been taken over by the people of vice.

I recently visited Newark, New Jersey, the city in which I grew up. If it wasn't for the police presence accompanying the religious festival I was attending, folks would not have visited that great city. Businesses are moving out and people are forsaking the cities because even law enforcement is ill-equipped to successfully deal with the growth of vice. When do we stop running and draw a line in the sand and say, "It stops here"?

Our military has been successful in stopping evil many times. It is not always deadly force that is the answer, but instead moral force that is needed. Why does evil scare us so much? Is it the fact that we are afraid to die, so that whatever makes that a possibility must be avoided? I love the words of the psalmist David: "I will fear no evil"! I am not suggesting the superficial phrase "No Fear" be our motto, because that is unrealistic in an evil world. To acknowledge the reality of fear without submitting to its power is the secret to overcoming it.

A virtuous person is a man or woman who is working from the inside out. They start with the heart and then are concerned with creature comforts. A knight or a warrior has honor, is noble, and is willing to sacrifice in the same way that our soldiers, Marines, sailors, and airmen do every day. I always felt safe on a military installation, not because there were weapons, but because there was an honor code by which people lived.

I don't want the world to be a police state, but instead a civilized place where people abide by the rule of law. Our American culture has, for the most part, conveniently forgotten the basic rules of right and wrong! Therefore, we find ourselves in a moral crisis regarding law and order due to the lack of resolve to implement morality. We hear the caveat that morality cannot be legislated, but the truth is that morality (not righteousness) has been legislated for years; laws concerning rape and murder bear this fact out. So the fallacy that declares government cannot legislate morality is uninformed.

Who does not want a society where there is true justice?

The criminal does not want that kind of society where there is true justice, which includes reparation for wrongs done, a topic not spoken about very often in our justice system. The tactic of true lawmakers who also possess compassion must include compassion for the victim as well as for the perpetrator. Justice without compassion is tyranny, and compassion without justice is permissiveness. Only people of character who have a virtuous disposition can achieve this level of fairness.

The world has been better and can achieve that high standard of living and dignity once again with the proper guidance and with real life examples. Everybody, for the most part, wants a fit body, but the cost of keeping it in shape is high. Most people want a good education, but not all are willing to make the necessary sacrifices to attain one. The same goes for a virtuous world—it will take hard work!

We, as Americans, can have such a world if we are willing to fight for it. What person has not had to struggle to achieve success? What nation has not had to make great sacrifices to remain competitive in the global economy? Human nature expects the positive results of success without paying the total price of sacrifice. This is neither reasonable nor realistic in the world in which we presently live. It was interesting to see the crowds respond in New York City on New Year's Eve one year to the song by John Lennon entitled *Imagine*, which sings about a world where there is utopian love. We, as Americans, love to dream but fall short on the effort part of seeing the dream being fulfilled. A moral utopia will require much work and sacrifice.

Goodness, although perceived as weakness at times, is really strength in disguise, just like quietness is sometimes perceived as shyness instead of seeing it as a characteristic of an insightful person who knows how to listen. Goodness, beauty, and truth are valuable traits for the soul of a nation. One of those three cannot override the others, one cannot overshadow the others, and none can be omitted.

Of these three virtues, goodness is oftentimes misunderstood. When we say that a person is good, saying for example that "he or she has a good heart," we can sometimes be insinuating that the person actually has a flaw or a manifestation of weakness. That goodness is not valued, but rather seen as something that is really there to cover that person's shyness, or lack of courage, or physical limitations. This only indicates we, as a culture, do not believe that goodness is the highest priority as a virtue. Truthtelling is valued as a virtue at times, but then devalued as an unnecessary scrupulous annoyance when it is inconvenient. One might ask, "What is truth or what is the truth?" The objective truth or the absolute truth is undeniable, but relative truth is more subjective and open to debate.

To distinguish these categories, consider the absolute truth that the sun is 93 million miles from earth. Someone may dispute that, but it is foolish to do so, because it's a proven fact and the truth. Yet relative truth, for example, is someone claiming that basketball is superior to baseball. That is a relative truth because one person subjectively values the results or the action in basketball, while another feels the same way about baseball.

Let's apply that truth to the concept of beauty. One man may believe he is married to the most beautiful woman in the world, and in his eyes, she is. Yet someone else can observe his wife, believe she is attractive, but is not ready to say that she is the most beautiful. That is because the beauty is subjective and is a matter of taste and opinion. Yet there is virtuous and creative beauty that is not subjective, but is valued and honored in almost all cultures because of its inherent excellence. Da Vinci's innovative sketches and Michelangelo's sculptures are considered beautiful by most people. In the realm of virtue, when someone goes out of his or her way to risk life and limb to save someone they don't even know who is trapped in a burning building, that is also considered a thing of beauty and nobility.

The eternal standard of beauty is silently but urgently

calling us to become better than we have thought ourselves to be. We spend time making ourselves and our homes beautiful rather than ugly. That state is preferred above deterioration and decay. What's more, the images of beauty and ugliness can create an imprint in our minds that lasts for the rest of our lives.

When I was a child, I ran across the decaying carcass of a dog and I can still see that picture in my mind 50 years later. Yet, I also have a mental picture of a sunset in the Philippines, which I captured with my camera, that is also imprinted in my mind for the rest of my life. That is the reason why we need to be exposed to beauty and limit the exposure to ugliness, and the same effect can be created by a virtuous person who carries out a noble act. It will be imprinted on our minds forever and actually be a source of inspiration to produce good ourselves.

If we focus on elegance, beauty, and goodness, we will be more apt to attain to those standards. If we behold baseness and crudeness, it will pull down our human spirit. We must have an antidote to that baseness or else our standards will begin to decline. That's why in the military we have formal events where we get dressed up in our military best. There's a time to get out of our field uniforms and dress up to see one another in a whole different light. I also urge police personnel to have an avocation that puts them in touch with the best of mankind and creation so that they are not overwhelmed by the misery and ugliness they often have to behold.

There is no doubt in the minds of all reasonable men that much of the nature in the world is beautiful, especially if it has been preserved to that end. If you go to the Grand Canyon, and you don't believe it's breathtaking, then there's something wrong. You may not like to hike the Canyon, or fly over the Canyon, or go through the travel trouble to get there, but once you see it, it's magnificent.

What's more, manmade things like cathedrals, palaces, castles, and other structures have evoked awe from complacent individuals when they beheld their beauty and stature. Even religious art pieces like the Sistine Chapel, which are not regarded for their religious value, are often valued for their beauty alone.

Hierarchy and structure contribute to the beauty of the universe; anarchy and disorder contribute to the desecration of the same. In order for something to receive praise, it must first be worthy of it. In order for something to be blameworthy, it must have an inherent defect and therefore be worthy of that description. Pollution would be an example, for something beautiful is marred by man's negligence and inattention to results.

We cannot find fault if someone does not possess the moral capacity to be virtuous; they would be true to their nature. We have seen throughout this book, however, that humans do possess the moral capacity as illustrated by the great feats that many men and women have attained throughout history. There are numerous concrete examples of the acquisition of virtue in numerous individuals on all continents since the beginning of time.

Throughout church history, there have been men and women, some from vile or deficient backgrounds, who, in cooperation with God's grace, made great personal transformations and impacted society for the good. We refer to them as saints of the church. I would urge you to do some simple research to see what I mean. Look at the lives and stories of people like St. Augustine of Hippo, St. Ambrose of Milan, St. Helena (Constantine's mother), St. Justin Martyr, St. Hildegard of Bingen, St. Albert the Great, and so many others who provide us examples and models of goodness, beauty, and truth in action. So what will we do, continue to make excuses or decide to take the path of virtue to make an impact in our own generation?

When I talk about heroes and villains to large groups, it is astonishing to see how difficult it is for some groups to choose real heroes and who cannot identify clearly-defined real villains. Exhibiting valor without virtue simply qualifies one as an incomplete hero. Yet this lack of attention to this important concept of virtue does not seem to faze some groups. This lack of being able to discriminate from the clear examples provided in these seminars, can make it difficult for police officers to exercise good judgment in moral matters when it really counts.

Therefore, moral exercises, not situational scenarios, are in order so as to strengthen the capacity to apply moral judgment. (I'm not talking about profiling, but about training through experience that will help professionals have a sense of what is a problem and what is not. Stereotypes are not healthy while one is pursuing moral development.) A person can be a "hero" at work, but neglect his or her family at home—does that not disqualify them from hero status? Integrity insists that the integration of these two spheres be consistent and the person does not deviate in either.

At this point, I can hear someone thinking, "That's not true. I may not be responsible in other areas of my life, but I am still a good cop or a good soldier!" That may be true where you are right now. My point is, however, that if you are struggling in one area of life and then are confronted with a new challenge in your work, it is quite possible you will not respond properly to that new challenge because you have not prepared yourself to do so. Again, let's return to a physical example. You may very well be able to lift 100 pounds and do it regularly. If you do not work out, however, and are confronted with the need to lift 150 pounds, you may fail because you were not prepared for the new weight.

If you have not been a good manager of your finances, it may not be a problem now. But what if your family is facing a financial crisis, and suddenly you have an opportunity to do something that would make you some money, even though it is against your organization's values or policy? If you have not worked to grow in virtue, you may take the risk and take the money, saying, "I'll only do it this once." Then, you do it again and again. Where did the problem start? It started long before you took the money. It started when you decided to be irresponsible with your personal finances.

You may have come from a poor family, or perhaps you never had any financial training. Do those realities exonerate you from walking with integrity by turning down the bribe or the other source of income? They do not. You are still responsible to grow in your ability to manage your money so that you can resist the temptation to take what's not really yours when you are in trouble.

Therefore, my answer to the question of whether or not character is critical is yes. Character counts in all of the above realms, and there are no excuses or passes for the valiant who do not wish to cultivate virtue. The reason why virtue has been a mystery is because it has not been desired or adhered to by the majority of citizens of Western cultures. The world would look quite different than it currently does if virtue was esteemed and valued, a topic I will cover in the Epilogue.

As we close this book, I want to reference the words of Jesus of Nazareth when He addressed the issue of virtue and moral development:

> Jesus said to his disciples: "A good tree does not bear rotten fruit, nor does a rotten tree bear good fruit. For every tree is known by its own fruit. For people do not pick figs from thornbushes, nor do they gather grapes from brambles. A good person out of the store of goodness in his heart produces good, but an evil person out of a store of evil produces evil; for from the fullness of the heart the mouth speaks (Luke 6:43-45 ABRE).
>
> "Why do you call me, 'Lord, Lord,' but not do what I command? I will show you what someone is like who comes to me, listens to my words, and acts on them. That one is like a man building a house, who

dug deeply and laid the foundation on rock; when the flood came, the river burst against that house but could not shake it because it had been well built. But the one who listens and does not act is like a person who built a house on the ground without a foundation. When the river burst against it, it collapsed at once and was completely destroyed" (Luke 6:47-49 ABRE).

In these ancient words, we see the importance of a long-term view toward moral development. Eventually, everyone will be tested and they will pass or fail the test according to how well they have prepared for that day of testing. Jesus pointed out the importance of working on the inner being for eventually what is in a person will come out of a person, in either actions or words.

I urge you to heed what Jesus said and build your house on the rock of goodness and virtue. It may take longer but in the long-run will pay great dividends. Jesus urged His listeners to find words to act on. That speaks to the need to have others speak into your development so that you can avoid the blind spots and exaggerated assessment of capability that may not be present in your life.

There is no better way to end this book than with those passages from Luke. I hope I have convinced you of the need and equipped you for the task of moral development. If I can help you in any way as we journey together, please write me and let me know how.

QUESTIONS FOR REFLECTION

1. Is truth arbitrary, relative or absolute when measuring it against natural law (look up the definition of natural law to make sure you understand the question)?

2. Can you define beauty or is it totally subjective? Are there any standards you can think of that apply to all of life?

3. What is good—is it just contrary to evil, or is it an entity in itself?

4. Are there such things as universals, i.e. standards that all can and should live by?

5. Is the declaration of human rights of 1948 (you can look this up on the Internet and quickly read it) requiring more from humans than they are capable of producing?

6. Why are there war crimes if truth is relative and there is no real right and wrong?

EPILOGUE

Virtue, the goal of moral development, has evaded civilization for the most part not because it is impossible, but because many have not made serious attempts to achieve it. The basic idea of this book is that it is a realistic and achievable but a neglected discipline that is especially important to those who are public servants in the military and police spheres of influence. Those who have tried to achieve moral development, and have been successful, have become the moral examples and heroes whose stories we have read and are made into movies. We usually view them as anomalies, but we are inspired after we read about or view their lives to aspire to loftier moral heights. They are anomalies not only because they are rare, however, but because they are not esteemed and emulated. We love their stories but don't really believe that their standard is attainable in our work.

What role does the family play in this formation? What about civil law? Do they share in the formation of character in society? Or is the law simply there to catch the vicious when they do wrong? Is it enough to be restrained or should there be a higher goal for one's behavior? I hope we can agree that there can be a higher goal than mediocrity or avoidance of punishment. When discussing ethics, it is easy to be negative and claim that our freedoms are being restricted. That is not the case. People are free to do the right thing, but cannot do anything they choose that may be void of moral goodness. I am working to change this mindset by offering hope that things can be very different than what we know today.

Some law enforcement and military personnel feel they

need to be "badder" than the bad boys (and girls). Reality shows and movies have painted a picture of the good guys who are hardly distinguishable from the bad guys. We need to provide better examples from which those who protect our freedoms can learn and grow. Our heroes are afraid to show any vulnerability and believe they are always under siege. I have been in that position, and today I work with police as their chaplain as they face evil on a regular basis.

If a person purchased an old house, which had a leaky roof, and hanging shingles, giving it attention could easily rectify the condition. The same is true in the ethical realm of virtue; most of the present moral condition in America is due to neglect! The old house is representative of one's moral life, which was never meant to remain in a state of ill repair, but instead to be restored to its original luster. Innocence is not the same as naiveté. When a child loses his or her innocence, it is not a thing to be celebrated.

Many of the children of America are losing their innocence too soon, due to the naivete` of their guardians and uninformed parents. "Too much, too soon" is the rule of thumb for modern moral development. When we expose our children to sexual issues too soon, it defiles their moral character, and blurs their moral judgment when making moral decisions in the future. There is a saying from a wise king who had problems with sexual promiscuity. He asked the question (some believe out of frustration), "How can a young man keep his way pure?" His answer is found in the simple explanation, "to heed (to obey) God's word!"

Moral formation starts very early in life. If you question children that have had violating experiences early in their lives, they will share with you the stories with reference to their wounds. If they were given good training and a trusted person violated that early formation, it is hard to rebuild or restore their trust again. "All the king's horses and all the king's men couldn't put Humpty together again!" There is an old saying that goes, "It is better to build children then to repair people." The building process is a grueling one, which takes many years. Children are not like chickens or crops, which are merely raised, but instead they must be carefully groomed and shaped into responsible citizens. This process does not happen by osmosis, but it happens intentionally.

"The apple does not fall far from the tree" is a saying that means the children will tend to be like the parents who trained and shaped them. This statement fails to take into account free will and genetics (nature, not just nurture). Children, like leaders, are born *and* made. They are not raised like hogs or some other domestic animal in an impersonal, inhumane way. Character is not predisposed as if there was a DNA clock that regulates one's behavior. There are a lot of determining factors, the least of which is economic status. Having personally been raised poor in the "projects" of Newark, New Jersey in the 1950s and 1960s, I have some firsthand experience and insight into the matter of one's environment limiting one's moral capacity. Virtue building is hard work, and unless there is an impetus and a great motivation for doing so, it is not being presently pursued in our American hedonistic culture.

I have committed my adult life to assist our law enforcement and military personnel engage the work of moral development. I continue to read and study, for I would like to think I am a scholar, but I also train and teach to help our men and women both to grasp the size of the task and then also to equip them to grow and develop. This book is part of my effort to reach out and convince you that we can grow in virtue. It is not a lost cause or beyond our reach. It will take work, and much dialogue in what is, today, a permissive, and tolerant society. Perhaps I am idealistic, but I have seen enough men and women "under fire" and seen them respond with grace and courage to have faith that we as a people are up to the task described in this book.

If I can help you or the organization you work for think

through what it will take to grow in virtue, please contact me using any of the sources listed at the end of this book. In the meantime, I hope you are inspired to get to work, and that you will get about the job of swimming in your peanut butter, so that together we may contribute our fair share to the moral improvement of our professional and national cultures.

APPENDIX

I have purposely omitted many references to Scripture since I desire this book to be used by all types of organizations that are not considered faith-based. Yet, I have made reference to some principles that emanate from the Judeo-Christian heritage of our country, which of course established the moral foundation for our laws and customs. In this Appendix, I include a list of references that you can examine and then apply in your own moral development or that of your organization or entity.

1. **Peer pressure** (1 Corinthians 15:33): "Do not be deceived: 'Bad company corrupts good morals.'"

2. **How to deal with evil** (Romans 12:21 NASB): "Do not be overcome by evil, but overcome evil with good."

3. **Long-term work of morality building** (Luke 6:46-49): "Why do you call me 'Lord, Lord,' and not do what I tell you? Everyone who comes to me and hears my words and does them, I will show you what he is like: he is like a man building a house, who dug deep and laid the foundation on the rock. And when a flood arose, the stream broke against that house and could not shake it, because it had been well built. But the one who hears and does not do them is like a man who built a house on the ground without a foundation. When the stream broke against it, immediately it fell, and the ruin of that house was great."

4. **The Ten Commandments** (Exodus 20:2-17 NKJV):

    1. "I am the Lord your God, who brought you out of the land of Egypt, out of the house of bondage. You shall have no other gods before Me.

    2. "You shall not make for yourself a carved image, or any likeness of anything that is in heaven above, or that is in the earth beneath, or that is in the water under the earth; you shall not bow down to them nor serve them. For I, the Lord your God, am a jealous God, visiting the iniquity of the fathers on the children to the third and fourth generations of those who hate Me, but showing mercy to thousands, to those who love Me and keep My Commandments.

    3. "You shall not take the name of the Lord your God in vain, for the Lord will not hold him guiltless who takes His name in vain.

    4. "Remember the Sabbath day, to keep it holy. Six days you shall labor and do all your work, but the seventh day is the Sabbath of the Lord your God. In it you shall do no work: you, nor your son, nor your daughter, nor your male servant, nor your female servant, nor your cattle, nor your stranger who is within your gates. For in six days the Lord made the heavens and the earth, the sea, and all that is in them, and rested the seventh day. Therefore the Lord blessed the Sabbath day and hallowed it.

    5. "Honor your father and your mother, that your days may be long upon the land which

the Lord your God is giving you.

6. "You shall not murder.

7. "You shall not commit adultery.

8. "You shall not steal.

9. "You shall not bear false witness against your neighbor.

10. "You shall not covet your neighbor's house; you shall not covet your neighbor's wife, nor his male servant, nor his female servant, nor his ox, nor his donkey, nor anything that is your neighbor's."

5. **The Beatitudes** (Matthew 5:1-12): And seeing the multitudes, He went up on a mountain, and when He was seated His disciples came to Him. Then He opened His mouth and taught them, saying: "Blessed are the poor in spirit, for theirs is the kingdom of heaven. Blessed are those who mourn, for they shall be comforted. Blessed are the meek, for they shall inherit the earth. Blessed are those who hunger and thirst for righteousness, for they shall be filled. Blessed are the merciful, for they shall obtain mercy. Blessed are the pure in heart, for they shall see God. Blessed are the peacemakers, for they shall be called sons of God. Blessed are those who are persecuted for righteousness' sake, for theirs is the kingdom of heaven. Blessed are you when they revile and persecute you, and say all kinds of evil against you falsely for My sake. Rejoice and be exceedingly glad, for great is your reward in heaven, for so they persecuted the prophets who were before you."

6. **Believers are salt and light** (Matthew 5:13-16): "You are the salt of the earth; but if the salt

loses its flavor, how shall it be seasoned? It is then good for nothing but to be thrown out and trampled underfoot by men. "You are the light of the world. A city that is set on a hill cannot be hidden. Nor do they light a lamp and put it under a basket, but on a lampstand, and it gives light to all who are in the house. Let your light so shine before men, that they may see your good works and glorify your Father in heaven."

7. **Christ fulfills the Law** (Matthew 5:17-20): "Do not think that I came to destroy the Law or the Prophets. I did not come to destroy but to fulfill. For assuredly, I say to you, till heaven and earth pass away, one jot or one tittle will by no means pass from the law till all is fulfilled. Whoever therefore breaks one of the least of these commandments, and teaches men so, shall be called least in the kingdom of heaven; but whoever does and teaches them, he shall be called great in the kingdom of heaven. For I say to you, that unless your righteousness exceeds the righteousness of the scribes and Pharisees, you will by no means enter the kingdom of heaven."

8. **Murder begins in the heart** (Matthew 5:21-26). "You have heard that it was said to those of old, 'You shall not murder, and whoever murders will be in danger of the judgment.' But I say to you that whoever is angry with his brother without a cause shall be in danger of the judgment. And whoever says to his brother, 'Raca!' shall be in danger of the council. But whoever says, 'You fool!' shall be in danger of hell fire. Therefore if you bring your gift to the altar, and there remember that your brother has something against

you, leave your gift there before the altar, and go your way. First be reconciled to your brother, and then come and offer your gift. Agree with your adversary quickly, while you are on the way with him, lest your adversary deliver you to the judge, the judge hand you over to the officer, and you be thrown into prison. Assuredly, I say to you, you will by no means get out of there till you have paid the last penny."

9. **Adultery in the heart** (Matthew 5:27-30): "You have heard that it was said to those of old, 'You shall not commit adultery.' But I say to you that whoever looks at a woman to lust for her has already committed adultery with her in his heart. If your right eye causes you to sin, pluck it out and cast it from you; for it is more profitable for you that one of your members perish, than for your whole body to be cast into hell. And if your right hand causes you to sin, cut it off and cast it from you; for it is more profitable for you that one of your members perish, than for your whole body to be cast into hell."

10. **Marriage is sacred and binding** (Matthew 5:31-32): "Furthermore it has been said, 'Whoever divorces his wife, let him give her a certificate of divorce.' But I say to you that whoever divorces his wife for any reason except sexual immorality causes her to commit adultery; and whoever marries a woman who is divorced commits adultery."

11. **Warning against making oaths** (Matthew 5:33-37): "Again you have heard that it was said to those of old, 'You shall not swear falsely, but shall perform your oaths to the Lord.' But I say to you, do not swear at all: neither by heaven, for

it is God's throne; nor by the earth, for it is His footstool; nor by Jerusalem, for it is the city of the great King. Nor shall you swear by your head, because you cannot make one hair white or black. But let your 'Yes' be 'Yes,' and your 'No,' 'No.' For whatever is more than these is from the evil one.'"

12. **Go the second mile** (Matthew 5:38-42): "You have heard that it was said, 'An eye for an eye and a tooth for a tooth.' But I tell you not to resist an evil person. But whoever slaps you on your right cheek, turn the other to him also. If anyone wants to sue you and take away your tunic, let him have your cloak also. And whoever compels you to go one mile, go with him two. Give to him who asks you, and from him who wants to borrow from you do not turn away."

13. **Love your enemies** (Matthew 5:43-48): "You have heard that it was said, 'You shall love your neighbor and hate your enemy.' But I say to you, love your enemies, bless those who curse you, do good to those who hate you, and pray for those who spitefully use you and persecute you, that you may be sons of your Father in heaven; for He makes His sun rise on the evil and on the good, and sends rain on the just and on the unjust. For if you love those who love you, what reward have you? Do not even the tax collectors do the same? And if you greet your brethren only, what do you do more than others? Do not even the tax collectors do so? Therefore you shall be perfect, just as your Father in heaven is perfect."

14. **Final judgment** (Hebrews 9:27 MEV): "As it is appointed for men to die once, but after this

comes the judgment."

15. **Accountability for life lived** (Matthew 25:14-30 MEV): "Again, the kingdom of heaven is like a man traveling into a far country, who called his own servants and entrusted his goods to them. To one he gave five talents, to another two, and to another one, to every man according to his ability. And immediately he took his journey. He who had received the five talents went and traded with them and made another five talents. So also, he who had received two gained another two. But he who had received one went and dug in the ground and hid his master's money.

"After a long time the master of those servants came and settled accounts with them. He who had received five talents came and brought the other five talents, saying, 'Master, you entrusted to me five talents. Look, I have gained five talents more.' His master said to him, 'Well done, you good and faithful servant. You have been faithful over a few things. I will make you ruler over many things. Enter the joy of your master.' He who had received two talents also came and said, 'Master, you entrusted me with two talents. See, I have gained two more talents besides them.' His master said to him, 'Well done, you good and faithful servant. You have been faithful over a few things. I will make you ruler over many things. Enter the joy of your master.'

"Then he who had received the one talent came and said, 'Master, I knew that you are a hard man, reaping where you did not sow, and gathering where you did not winnow. So I was afraid, and went and hid your talent in the ground. Here you have what is yours.' His master answered, 'You wicked and slothful servant! You knew that I reap where I have not sown, and gather where I have not winnowed. Then you ought to have given my money to the bankers, and at my coming I should have received what was my own with interest.

"'So take the talent from him, and give it to him who has ten talents. For to everyone who has will more be given, and he will have an abundance. But from him who has nothing, even what he has will be taken away. And throw the unprofitable servant into outer darkness, where there will be weeping and gnashing of teeth.'"

16. **The Judgment of the nations** (Matthew 25:31-46 NASB): "When the Son of Man comes in His glory, and all the holy angels with Him, then He will sit on the throne of His glory. Before Him will be gathered all nations, and He will separate them one from another as a shepherd separates his sheep from the goats. He will set the sheep at His right hand, but the goats at the left.

"Then the King will say to those at His right hand, 'Come, you blessed of My Father, inherit the kingdom prepared for you since the foundation of the world. For I was hungry and you gave Me food, I was thirsty and you gave Me drink, I was a stranger and you took Me in. I was naked and you clothed Me, I was sick and you visited Me, I was in prison and you came to Me.'

"Then the righteous will answer Him, 'Lord, when did we see You hungry and feed You, or thirsty and give You drink? When did we see You a stranger and take You in, or naked and clothe You? And when did we see You sick or in prison and come to You?' "The King will answer, 'Truly I say to you, as you have done it for one of the least of these brothers of Mine, you have done it for Me.'

"Then He will say to those at the left hand, 'Depart from Me, you cursed, into the eternal fire, prepared for the devil and his angels. For I was hungry and you gave Me no food, I was thirsty and you gave Me no drink, I was a stranger and you did not take Me in, I was naked and you did not clothe Me, I was sick and in prison and you did not visit Me.'

"Then they also will answer Him, 'Lord, when did we see You hungry or thirsty or a stranger or naked or sick or in prison, and did not serve You?' "He will answer, 'Truly I say to you, as you did it not for one of the least of these, you did it not for Me.' "And they will go away into eternal punishment, but the righteous into eternal life."

17. **Love** (1 Corinthians 13 MEV): "If I speak with the tongues of men and of angels, and have not love, I have become as sounding brass or a clanging cymbal. If I have the gift of prophecy, and understand all mysteries and all knowledge, and if I have all faith, so that I could remove mountains, and have not love, I am nothing. If I give all my goods to feed the poor, and if I give my body to be burned, and have not love, it profits me nothing.

Love suffers long and is kind; love envies not; love flaunts not itself and is not puffed up, does not behave itself improperly, seeks not its own, is not easily provoked, thinks no evil; rejoices not in iniquity, but rejoices in the truth; bears all things, believes all things, hopes all things, and endures all things.

Love never fails. But if there are prophecies, they shall fail; if there are tongues, they shall cease; and if there is knowledge, it shall vanish. For we know in part, and we prophesy in part. But when that which is perfect comes, then that which is imperfect shall pass away. When I was a child, I spoke as a child, I understood as a child, and I thought as a child. But when I became a man, I put away childish things. For now we see as through a glass, dimly, but then, face to face. Now I know in part, but then I shall know, even as I also am known. So now abide faith, hope, and love, these three. But the greatest of these is love.

18. **Warning against adultery** (Proverbs 5 MEV):

¹My son, attend to my wisdom,
    and bow your ear to my understanding,
²that you may regard discretion,
    and that your lips may keep knowledge.
³For the lips of an immoral woman drip as a
    honeycomb,
    and her mouth is smoother than oil.
⁴But her end is bitter as wormwood,
    sharp as a two-edged sword.
⁵Her feet go down to death,
    her steps take hold of Sheol.

⁶She does not ponder the path of life;
   her ways are unstable, and she does not know it.
⁷Hear me now therefore, O children,
   and do not depart from the words of my mouth.
⁸Remove your way far from her,
   and do not go near the door of her house,
⁹lest you give your honor to others,
   and your years to the cruel;
¹⁰lest strangers be filled with your wealth,
   and your labors go to the house of a stranger;
¹¹and you mourn at the last,
   when your flesh and your body are consumed,
¹²and say, "How I have hated instruction,
   and my heart despised reproof!
¹³And I have not obeyed the voice of my teachers,
   nor inclined my ear to those who instructed me!
¹⁴I was almost in utter ruin
   in the midst of the congregation and assembly."
¹⁵Drink waters out of your own cistern,
   and running waters out of your own well.
¹⁶Should your fountains be dispersed abroad,
   streams of water in the streets?
¹⁷Let them be only your own,
   and not for strangers with you.
¹⁸Let your fountain be blessed,
   and rejoice with the wife of your youth.
¹⁹Let her be as the loving deer and pleasant doe;
   let her breasts satisfy you at all times;
   and always be enraptured with her love.
²⁰Why should you, my son, be intoxicated by an
      immoral woman,
   and embrace the bosom of a seductress?
²¹For the ways of man are before the eyes of the
      Lord,

and He ponders all his goings.
²²His own iniquities entrap the wicked himself,
and he is snared in the cords of his sins.
²³He will die for lack of instruction,
and in the greatness of his folly he will go
astray.

19. **Warning against pledges** (Proverbs 6:1-5 MEV)

¹My son, if you put up a security for your friend,
if you have shaken hands with a stranger,
²you are snared with the words of your mouth;
you are taken with the words of your mouth.
³Do this now, my son, and deliver yourself;
when you have come into the hand of your
friend,
go and humble yourself;
plead with your friend.
⁴Give no sleep to your eyes,
nor slumber to your eyelids.
⁵Deliver yourself as a doe from the hand of the
hunter,
and as a bird from the hand of the fowler.

20. **The folly of idleness** (Proverbs 6:6-11)

⁶Go to the ant, you sluggard!
Consider her ways and be wise.
⁷Which, having no guide,
overseer, or ruler,
⁸provides her bread in the summer,
and gathers her food in the harvest.
⁹How long will you sleep, O sluggard?
When will you arise out of your sleep?
¹⁰Yet a little sleep, a little slumber,
a little folding of the hands to sleep—
¹¹so will your poverty come upon you like a stalker,

and your need as an armed man.

21. **The wicked man** (Proverbs 6:12-19)

[12]A wayward person, a wicked man,
    walks with a perverse mouth.
[13]He winks with his eyes,
    he signals with his feet,
    he motions with his fingers;
[14]perversity is in his heart,
    he devises mischief continually, he sows discord.
[15]Therefore his calamity will come suddenly;
    in a moment he will be broken without remedy.
[16]These six things the Lord hates,
    yes, seven are an abomination to him:
[17]a proud look,
    a lying tongue,
    and hands that shed innocent blood,
[18]a heart that devises wicked imaginations,
    feet that are swift in running to mischief,
[19]a false witness who speaks lies,
    and he who sows discord among brethren.

22. **Warning against adultery** (Proverbs 6:20-35)

[20]My son, keep your father's commandment,
    and do not forsake the instruction of your mother.
[21]Bind them continually upon your heart,
    and tie them around your neck.
[22]When you go, they will lead you;
    when you sleep, they will keep you;
    and when you awake, they will speak with you.
[23]For the commandment is a lamp, and the law
    is light;
    and reproofs of instruction are the way of life,
[24]to keep you from the evil woman,

from the flattery of the tongue of a seductress.
[25]Do not lust after her beauty in your heart,
    nor let her allure you with her eyelids.
[26]For by means of a harlot a man is reduced to a
    piece of bread,
    and the adulteress will prey upon his precious
    life.
[27]Can a man take fire in his bosom,
    and his clothes not be burned?
[28]Can one walk upon hot coals,
    and his feet not be burned?
[29]So he who goes in to his neighbor's wife;
    whoever touches her will not be innocent.
[30]Men do not despise a thief if he steals
    to satisfy himself when he is hungry.
[31]But if he is found, he will restore sevenfold;
    he will give all the substance of his house.
[32]But whoever commits adultery with a woman
lacks understanding;
    he who does it destroys his own soul.
[33]A wound and dishonor will he get,
    and his reproach will not be wiped away.
[34]For jealousy is the rage of a man;
    therefore he will not spare in the day of
    vengeance.
[35]He will not regard any ransom,
    nor will he rest content, though you give
    many gifts.

23. **Beware of the adulteress** (Proverbs 7:1 MEV)

[1]My son, keep my words,
    and lay up my commandments within you.
[2]Keep my commandments and live,
    and my teaching as the apple of your eye.
[3]Bind them on your fingers;

write them on the tablet of your heart.
⁴Say to wisdom, "You are my sister,"
   and call understanding your kinswoman,
⁵that they may keep you from the immoral woman,
   from the seductress who flatters with her words.
⁶For at the window of my house
   I looked through my casement,
⁷and saw among the simple ones,
   I discerned among the youths,
   a young man void of understanding,
⁸passing through the street near her corner;
   and he went the way to her house
⁹in the twilight, in the evening,
   in the black and dark night.
¹⁰And there a woman met him,
   with the attire of a harlot, and subtle of heart.
¹¹She is loud and stubborn;
   her feet do not abide in her house.
¹²Now she is without, now in the streets,
   and lies in wait at every corner.
¹³So she caught him, and kissed him;
   and with an impudent face said to him:
¹⁴"I have peace offerings with me;
   this day have I paid my vows.
¹⁵Therefore I came out to meet you,
   diligently to seek your face, and I have found
      you.
¹⁶I have decked my bed with coverings of tapestry,
   with carved works, with fine linen of Egypt.
¹⁷I have perfumed my bed
   with myrrh, aloes, and cinnamon.
¹⁸Come, let us take our fill of love until the morning;
   let us solace ourselves with love.
¹⁹For my husband is not at home;

he has gone on a long journey;
²⁰he has taken a bag of money with him,
and will come home at the day appointed."
²¹With her enticing speech she caused him to yield,
with the flattering of her lips she seduced him.
²²He went after her straightway,
as an ox goes to the slaughter,
or as a fool to the correction of the stocks,
²³until a dart struck through his liver.
As a bird hastens to the snare,
he did not know that it would cost him his life.
²⁴Listen to me now therefore, O children,
and attend to the words of my mouth:
²⁵do not let your heart turn aside to her ways,
do not go astray in her paths;
²⁶for she has cast down many wounded,
and many strong men have been slain by her.
²⁷Her house is the way to Sheol,
going down to the chambers of death.

REFERENCES

1. Demarco, Dr. Donald. *The Many Faces of Virtue.* Emmaus Road Publishing: (2000)
2. Einstein, Albert (1939), *Science and Religion.* Retrieved from http://www.panarchy.org/einstein/science.religion.1939.html
3. The Gnostic Muse. *Joan of Arc: In Her Own Words.* Retrieved from http://www.gnosticmuse.com/joan-of-arc/.
4. Kelly, Rev. Bennet, C.P. *Saint Joseph Baltimore Catechism: The Truths of our Catholic Faith Clearly Explained and Illustrated* (Official Revised Version). Catholic Book Publishing: New York (1954).
5. Kohlberg, Lawrence (1971), *Stages of Moral Development.* Retrieved from http://info.psu.edu.sa/psu/maths/Stages%20of%20Moral%20Development%20According%20to%20Kohlberg.pdf
6. Mansfield, Stephen. *Never Give In: The Extraordinary Character of Winston Churchill.* Cumberland House Publishing: (2002).

WHO IS

FATHER

MICHAEL PACELLA?

Father Michael was called to God's service while serving in the Navy off the coast of Vietnam. He subsequently entered active ministry in 1974, combining practical mission service with his theological education. He became the founding pastor of New London (CT) Covenant Church, where he also established the Coastline Christian Academy. In 1995 Father Michael entered the Army Reserve, and in 1997 he was called back to military ministry, departing Covenant Church and entering the Active Army as a Chaplain to serve in Rhode Island, Fort Bragg, NC, Korea and Fort Eusis, VA, where he was awarded instructor of the year. He exited the military in 2005.

Father Michael entered the CEC in 2002, and resigned from the Army the following year to establish the Church of the Blessed Redeemer, while resuming the teaching ministry he had pursued in the Army. Over the next ten years, Father Michael taught primarily at the College of William and Mary, at Hampton University, St Leo's College, Regents University, and the Kings College at Jamestown, where he was the primary Theology and Ethics professor in the Seminary school. At the same time, he served as police chaplain for the College of William and Mary, and was assigned to Saint Andrews Church in Petersburg VA.

Father Michael presented academic papers at international forums at Cambridge (2009), Thessalonica (2012) and Athens (2013). In 2013, Father Michael was accepted as a doctoral candidate into the Institute for Orthodox Christian Studies at Cambridge, where he is a full member of the Cambridge Theological Federation. He has received All but Dissertation (ABD) status toward his PhD, and his final PhD award is pending. Father Michael was selected to present a paper on Saint Gregory Palamas at the 17th International Conference on Patristic Studies at Oxford in the UK in 2015.

Father Michael has extensive academic credentials, holding a Masters in Divinity from Yale University and a Masters in Theology from Harvard, as well as his current work at Cambridge. He continues his teaching ministry at Saint Michael's Seminary of the CEC, and will complete his doctoral studies in 2019.

TO CONTACT
FATHER MICHAEL PACELLA,
PLEASE WRITE:

Father Michael Pacella III
Saint Michael and All Angels Church
Williamsburg, Virginia 23185
757.784.1904

saintmichaelschurch14@gmail.com

Made in the USA
Middletown, DE
18 July 2020